This book is due for return on or before the last date shown below.

SCOTNOTES

Study guides to major Scottish writers and literary texts

Produced by the Schools and Further Education Committee
of the Association for Scottish Literary Studies

Series Editors

Lorna Borrowman Smith, Wallace High School, Stirling
Dr Elaine Petrie, Falkirk College of Further and Higher
Education

Editorial Board

Cover design by Linda Cochrane

THE ASSOCIATION FOR SCOTTISH LITERARY STUDIES aims to promote the study, teaching and writing of Scottish literature, and to further the study of the languages of Scotland.

To these ends, the ASLS publishes works of Scottish literature, literary criticism in *Scottish Literary Journal*, scholarly studies of language in *Scottish Language*, and in-depth reviews of Scottish books in *SLJ Supplements*. It also publishes *New Writing Scotland*, an annual anthology of new poetry, drama and short fiction, in Scots, English and Gaelic, by Scottish writers. ASLS has also prepared a range of teaching materials covering Scottish language and literature for use in schools.

All the above publications, except for the teaching materials, are available as a single 'package', in return for an annual subscription. Enquiries should be sent to: ASLS, c/o Department of Scottish History, University of Glasgow, 9 University Gardens, Glasgow G12 8QH, telephone 0141 330 5309 (e-mail: cmc@arts. gla.ac.uk).

SCOTNOTES
Number 15

The Poetry of Hugh MacDiarmid

Alan Riach

Association for Scottish Literary Studies 1999

Published by
Association for Scottish Literary Studies
c/o Department of Scottish History
University of Glasgow
9 University Gardens
Glasgow G12 8QH

First published 1999

A CIP catalogue for this title is available from the British Library

ISBN 0 948877 40 5

Subsidised by

Typeset by Roger Booth Associates, Hassocks, West Sussex

CONTENTS

Acknowledgements

I am very grateful to the Institute for Advanced Studies in the Humanities at the University of Edinburgh, where I held visiting fellowships in 1995 and 1996–97; to the staff of the National Library of Scotland, the University of Edinburgh Library, the Mitchell Library (Glasgow) and the University of Waikato Library; to the University of Waikato School of Humanities Research Committee, for their support of my work on MacDiarmid; to Carcanet Press for their continuing commitment to making MacDiarmid available in appropriate magnitude at last; and to my colleagues at the University of Waikato, Professor Marshall Walker and Dr Jan Pilditch, for unfailing professional sustenance. The Frontispiece, 'Head of Poet' (1964) by William Johnstone, is reproduced by permission of the owner and I would like to acknowledge the generosity of the late John Cunningham for his gift of it. The song-setting by F.G. Scott is reprinted by permission of Roberton Publications. My understanding of MacDiarmid owes much to my friends and teachers and in particular I must thank T.J. Cribb, C.T. Larsen and Peter McCarey. More than gratitude is due to my wife Rae. This little book is an introduction to the work of one of the great poets of the twentieth century. I would like to dedicate it to two of the innocents yet to encounter him.

For
James Garton Riach and David John Riach
'larks in the clear air'

A Note on the Texts

Page numbers refer to Hugh MacDiarmid, *Selected Poems*, edited by Alan Riach and Michael Grieve (Harmondsworth: Penguin Books, 1994). References to *A Drunk Man Looks at the Thistle* are by line number as per this selection. Poems not included in this selection may be found in *The Complete Poems of Hugh MacDiarmid*, edited by Michael Grieve and W.R. Aitken (Manchester: Carcanet, 1993–94). Other important texts are listed in the bibliography at the end of the book.

Introduction

Hugh MacDiarmid is one of the monuments. He commands attention for two reasons: first, he wrote great poetry, and second, his life's work was of historic importance.

His reputation remains controversial. The publisher Joy Hendry called him 'the most important single figure in Scottish life in the twentieth century'. The novelist Irvine Welsh said he was 'a symbol of all that's perfectly hideous in Scotland'.

You'll have to make up your own mind about him.

This little book is mainly concerned to introduce MacDiarmid's work in general and then to read closely a number of particular poems, to point out some of the places where you might catch the bus.

Like him or loathe him, MacDiarmid's work is of real magnitude. The journalist Andrew Marr once wrote: 'MacDiarmid's poetry remains a vast and little-colonised continent of wonders, glittering views and strange formations, which everyone with the requisite supply of synapses and a little common courage should visit.' It opens more doors than that of any other major modern writer. It engages different disciplines again and again: science, biology, philosophy, geology, linguistics, politics, music, art, economics, and others. And just as no subject is foreign to his writing, his writing adopts a range of different forms: lyric, epic, satire, rhapsody, elegy. Its foremost quality is variety.

Nevertheless, his poems inhabit three principal areas of sensibility. He is uniquely capable of expressing wonder and mystery, while enquiring into them carefully; he is deeply concerned with political issues and social justice, so he is a passionate satirist; and he is ultimately a poet of hope, expressing a hard-earned vision of the individual, society and nation, and what might be made of them.

But before we engage with the poetry more closely, we should find out something of the world from which it emerged.

Hugh MacDiarmid: A Short Biography
Hugh MacDiarmid was the pseudonym of Christopher Murray Grieve (1892–1978).

He was born in Langholm, Dumfriesshire, near the English border, and trained as a teacher, but after his father's death he became a journalist in Edinburgh and Wales. He volunteered for service in World War I, joining the Royal Army Medical Corps in Salonika in Greece, and France. After recovering from cerebral malaria, he was demobbed and returned to a career in journalism in Scotland, settling in Montrose with his first wife Margaret, and starting a family in the 1920s.

Abandoning attempts to write Georgian poetry in English, he launched the Scottish Literary Renaissance movement, intending to dissociate Scotland from Victorian sentimentalism and to direct the culture towards modernist and European tendencies and developments. He knew Joseph Conrad, W.B. Yeats, T.S. Eliot and Ezra Pound. A founder of the National Party of Scotland in 1928, his writing was often outrageously provocative. There was a conservative backlash and after a brief time in London as editor of the radio journal *Vox*, his personal life was irreparably disrupted.

Estranged from his first wife and family, he moved to the Shetland Islands with his second wife Valda Trevlyn and their young son, where he was based in the 1930s, surviving poverty, isolation and, in 1935, physical and mental breakdown. Yet he was producing poetry of political conviction and renewed philosophical depth. In 1934, he had joined the Communist Party of Great Britain (CPGB) while advocating separatism for Scotland. The 'First Hymn to Lenin' (1931) was followed by *Stony Limits* (1935), with the great meditative poem 'On a Raised Beach' at its centre.

'On a Raised Beach' is the central poem of MacDiarmid's career but it is difficult: a philosophical enquiry charged with emotion, located on a storm beach in the Shetland Islands, 410 lines intensely focused on the relation between language and reality. In this book, we can't give it the space it requires, but a detailed analysis of its argument and structure is in Alan Riach's essay 'The Idea of Order and "On a Raised Beach"' (the reference is in the bibliography).

In the Shetland years, his output was prodigious. A vituperative book-length poem in support of the International Brigade and the Republicans of Spain, *The Battle Continues*, was written in the late 1930s, praising the democratic socialist side in the Spanish Civil War, and deriding the pro-Franco poet Roy Campbell. And there were other books of prose, or poetry and prose combined, including an autobiography, *Lucky Poet* (1943).

After work during World War II in a munitions factory in Glasgow and on boats on the Clyde, MacDiarmid and his wife settled in a cottage near Biggar, Lanarkshire, again in the Scottish borders, where they lived from 1951 until his death in 1978. While in the Shetlands, he had started work on an endless poem on an epic scale, dealing with the relations between language, poetry and imperialism, parts of which were published as *In Memoriam James Joyce* (1955) and *The Kind of Poetry I Want* (1961). He continued to be outspoken in public and print, writing numerous verses and articles for journals, newspapers and magazines. He was well known as a broadcaster, public speaker, occasional journalist and controversial essayist. He stood as a Communist candidate against the Conservative Prime Minister Sir Alec Douglas-Home in the general election of 1964. After Douglas-Home was returned to office, MacDiarmid and the CPGB took him to court, arguing that access to television, radio and other media enjoyed by the Conservative Party and the Prime Minister was denied the smaller parties, and therefore modes of persuasion and open debate gave the bigger parties an unfair advantage.

Meanwhile, critical recognition of MacDiarmid's poetry had been growing internationally. The first edition of his *Complete Poems* was published in two volumes in 1978. Since his death, his literary and political influence has remained incalculable.

MacDiarmid's work is the principal means by which it became possible to represent Scotland, nationally and internationally, in recognisably modern ways.

But this bare summary of his life and work should be complemented by a sense of its complexity and moment.

The name 'Hugh M'Diarmid' first appeared in 1922, the great year of literary modernism, in which T.S. Eliot's *The Waste Land* and James Joyce's *Ulysses* were published. It became associated with two books of intense lyric poems in Scots and the long, satiric and discursive poem on national identity, *A Drunk Man Looks at the Thistle* (1926). For many readers, the early short poems in Scots are MacDiarmid's greatest achievement. For exemplary detailed readings of the most famous ('The Bonnie Broukit Bairn', 'Empty Vessel', 'The Innumerable Christ', 'The Watergaw' and 'The Eemis Stane'), you should refer to Kenneth Buthlay's essay 'The Appreciation of the Golden Lyric'. For further study of *A Drunk Man*, Buthlay's annotated edition is indispensable. (You'll find the references in the bibliography.)

At the same time as MacDiarmid was producing these poems, C.M. Grieve was writing innumerable articles for daily and weekly newspapers throughout Scotland, and educational and literary journals both in Scotland and England through the 1920s and into the 1930s. At this time, MacDiarmid/Grieve was uniquely qualified to initiate the Scottish Literary Renaissance movement, for he combined in himself at least four major areas of experience and knowledge nobody else possessed in the same balance.

(1) He was acutely aware of the modern movement in literature internationally. He knew the significance of Eliot and Joyce, and saw his own literary effort in relation to theirs. He was aware of a new movement happening in the arts generally. He realised that the disruptive and revisionary art of Picasso and the deliberately shocking music of Stravinsky and Schoenberg were related in this artistic revolution.

(2) He was marinated in the language and idiom of Scots, the rural speech he had grown up with. Scots was the tongue of his school playground; English was alien, to be learned and used in the classroom or 'polite' society. Speaking English was 'speaking *fine*'. In the country, the rural traditions and farming communities preserved and actively used Scots. Wry understanding of the animal aspects of being human and an appetite for comedy alien to genteel idioms were fundamental to that linguistic inheritance. Like Joyce, MacDiarmid could interrogate Victorian conventions of sexual morality by applying subversive and celebrative comedy, but unlike Joyce, he could do so in a vernacular language.

(3) Scots was predominantly an oral language. Its written forms had degenerated since the death of Burns. It was too familiarly used in sentimental homilies: comic, domestic and 'characterful'. But MacDiarmid saw how it might be linked to the experimental uses of language in modern writing, not only in Joyce and Eliot, but in Wallace Stevens, William Carlos Williams, Gertrude Stein and Edith Sitwell, the Dadaists, and the 'Landsmaal' movement in Norway, where a national language was being recreated for explicitly nationalist purposes. MacDiarmid's Scots is to do with energy, charge, chill and surprise; in his early lyrics it is deliberately made strange or 'defamiliarised'. For MacDiarmid, in literary and political terms, Scots was a weapon. It was *both* an idiom of speech (often used spontaneously, so it could move fluently and quickly) *and* an unusual form of written language which, as writing, drew attention to its own artifice (or artificiality, in the sense of being a 'made thing' which, consequently, could slow one's reading down).

For instance, a poem like 'The Eemis Stane' (pp.14–15) uses an idiom of vernacular Scots easily translated into English ('my eerie memories fa' ... so's I couldna read / The words cut oot i' the stane'), but also employs words and phrases from the dictionary ('the how-dumb-deid o' the cauld hairst nicht'). The effect is both intimate and strange, extremely familiar (as if you've grown up with these sounds and idioms) and weirdly incomprehensible (especially if, like many of MacDiarmid's readers, you've never seen such words on a page before). This is what gives a deeper authority to his attempts to express the ineffable.

After his experiments with Scots MacDiarmid was able to use forms of English that seemed equally strange, and from there to develop 'a vision of world language' in his later work – not any single national language imposed globally or a self-consciously constructed one such as Esperanto – but an internationally understandable multiplicity of tongues. His 'vision' was what this might be: not an incomprehensible babble, but an imagined harmony of interrelation.

(4) When he returned to Scotland after World War I, MacDiarmid began to look into the cultural history of his own country. Scottish writers have often rejected the idea that the economic authority of London in the British state signified an equivalent cultural status, but the relation between cultural and economic power has always been problematic. MacDiarmid grew up in a world where the border ballads would have been familiar, but the literary, linguistic and cultural history of Scotland was much more obscure and difficult to find out about than it is today. So MacDiarmid came to understand the historical consequences of the suppression of independent Scottish traditions and the rise of English to a position of dominance. He became aware of the interconnections between literary, cultural and political identity.

Bringing into focus these four areas of his sensibility in the early 1920s – concerns (1) with the international literary and cultural avant-garde, (2) with the vernacular idiom of Scots, (3) with its literary potential and (4) with the politics of nation and class – MacDiarmid was in a crucial position to crystallise and hold them at the axis of his writing. This is the position from which he embarked at the outset of his career.

MacDiarmid and the Modern Movement: International Themes and Contexts

The modern movement was characterised by the shock of the new. Often ancient and traditional themes or stories were shockingly reinvented for a modern sensibility, like those of Joyce's Homer, relocated from ancient Greece to Dublin, 1904, removed from their original habitat and denaturalised.

The introduction of ancient pagan, African or Oriental art forms to the West in the nineteenth century had been considered essentially anthropological or archaeological, but in the modern movement such art began to be considered as art. Western art examined the so-called 'primitive' bases of its own creativity (the darker side of the 'classical' worlds of Greece and Rome).

By doing so, it called attention to its own modes of production and thereby politicised its relation with its readers or audience. Art was no longer defined, comprehensive and closed (like a great Victorian novel, a well-made sonnet or a five-act play), but turned jagged, fragmentary, disrupted by meanings that cut across its own coherence. In *The Waste Land*, T.S. Eliot describes his own poetry when he says: 'These fragments I have shored against my ruins.'

Ultimate authority (whether an imperial standard or the Christian deity) was in question. The reader of Eliot or Joyce, the audience for Brecht, Picasso or Stravinsky, had to construct meaning from the artist's work, and that act of participation could only be made by choice.

This combination of overt artifice and subtle suggestion is illustrated by the frontispiece to this book: William Johnstone's 'Head of Poet'. It's recognisably a depiction of MacDiarmid, but it's also, blatantly, a few brush-strokes of boldness and subtle texture, exhibiting its own material formation.

The major English-language writers of the modern movement were exiles, keenly aware of displacement and alienation in their own lives and hypersensitive to the effects of such conditions upon their language. As writers of English, the international language of the modern world, they were especially attuned to its ambivalent character: it was both the language of colonial and imperial oppression and the language which united the different peoples of the Empire. Use of English, understanding its variety as well as its subtleties and nuances, was a political question for every one of them: the Americans Eliot and Pound, the Irishmen Yeats and Joyce, the Welshman Dylan Thomas, the Pole Joseph Conrad, the New Zealander Katherine Mansfield. For each writer, and also for important English modernist writers like Virginia Woolf or Edith Sitwell, the language was never to be taken for granted. It was, in a sense, an acquired tongue, a language to be learned, a means by which the world could be defamiliarised, made strange, looked at fresh or even, perhaps, changed.

The experimental modernism of MacDiarmid's early lyrics distinguishes them from the poems being written in Scots at the time by language archaeologists like Lewis Spence or vernacular dialect poets like Charles Murray, David Rorie, Violet Jacob or Marion Angus. The work of these poets could be accomplished and moving or full of comic immediacy, but the distinction of

MacDiarmid's work was that it embraced the most radical ideas to have emerged from the nineteenth century, and particularly the work of three men: Freud in psychology, Marx in economic and political theory, and Nietzsche in philosophy. They influenced all the great modernists and their principal ideas have so deeply and pervasively affected what is taken for granted today that it's easy to overlook their specific importance and to forget how shockingly new they were. Let's consider some of MacDiarmid's poems with reference to them.

Sigmund Freud (1856–1939) is associated with a cluster of related ideas: the significance of sexuality in the individual, the sexual tensions within the structure of the family, the information coded in dreams and the buried meanings accessible in the unconscious and the imagination in the form of symbolism.

Intense sexuality and wild leaps of symbolic imagery characterise many of MacDiarmid's early Scots lyrics. 'In the Hedge-Back' evokes a sexual encounter so shattering that the earth is all but destroyed by it; there are 'The Scarlet Woman', 'The Frightened Bride' and 'The Love-sick Lass' (p.17). The lover's feeling as he looks on his beloved in 'Wheesht, Wheesht' (p.16) is unnervingly ambiguous about the 'lust o' lovin'' coming to an end: is the beloved asleep or dead? 'Sabine' is equally disturbing in its terrifically compressed evocation of intense sexuality in the context of the conventional morality of small-town Scotland.

All of these poems use dense Scots phrases which crack open tentative but intense moments of perception and understanding. In Freudian terms, the language reveals what it seems to conceal. They are much more subtle texts than many others of the modern movement equally compelled by Freud, such as D.H. Lawrence's *Fantasia of the Unconscious* or *Women in Love*. In 'The Watergaw' (p.9) the poet recollects the 'last wild look' given on the point of death by (most probably) his father. The 'foolish licht' of the shivering rainbow beyond the downpour heralds realisation, but knowledge of what 'your look meant then' is only cautiously assumed: 'I think that mebbe at last I ken'. That 'at last' signifies the realisation made in each individual reading of the poem: an adult remembering when he was still a teenager, at the moment of his father's death. The dead father's 'wild look' must always be a question: it's asking what will happen in the future he cannot know. MacDiarmid's mysterious, shimmering answer is the poem itself. As he says in 'At My Father's Grave' (p.141): 'A livin' man upon a deid man thinks / And ony sma'er thocht's impossible.'

The work of **Karl Marx (1818–83)** introduced ways of understanding the operation of social classes, which are almost universally accepted. The accepted meanings of words and phrases like class (and class struggle, class warfare, class consciousness), proletariat, ideology, alienation and the fetishism of commodities all derive from Marx. It's now generally assumed that 'the mode of production of material life conditions the social, political and intellectual life process in general'. MacDiarmid's self-proclaimed Marxism has often been deemed idiosyncratic but when we come to discuss the political themes in his poems we shall see how appropriate the term is.

Let's look at one example briefly. A note prefixed to the poem 'To My Friend the Late Beatrice Hastings' (pp.300–3) explains that it was written partly in answer to a friend's request for help for her son, who was writing a school essay on religion and 'youth today'.

The poem is an argument, asking questions and analysing the nature of those questions in Marxist terms, recognising the 'need for metaphysics' ('metaphysics' simply means 'beyond' physics, something more than the material universe) but contending that this need has its roots in the material conditions of everyday life, and historical roots which nourish it. MacDiarmid's conclusion is Marxist in its refusal to admit 'metaphysical' answers to material problems (religion is not a remedy for poverty) and in its historical-materialist method of analysing the recurrence of 'metaphysical need' in different forms of expression: it is important to understand how certain ideas 'return, out of what causes, / In what form and under what circumstances'. The specific contexts of any supposedly 'universal' ideas must be examined.

The principal thoughts associated with the work of the philosopher **Friedrich Nietzsche (1844–1900)** are closely interwoven with MacDiarmid's poetry and beliefs. 'God is dead' wrote Nietzsche in the 1880s, and in a sense the twentieth century began then. So much 'was built upon this faith', belief in God, Nietzsche said, so much was 'propped up by it', that its abandonment has had consequences far beyond 'the multitude's capacity for comprehension'. MacDiarmid's early poem 'The Fool' (p.7) (the title suggests Nietzsche's spokesman, 'The Madman' in *The Gay Science*) is a bitter distillation of the matter:

> He said that he was God.
>   'We are well met,' I cried,
> 'I've always hoped I should
>   Meet God before I died.'

> I slew him then and cast
> His corpse into a pool,
> — But how I wish he had
> Indeed been God, the fool!

The question returns more hauntingly in 'Sea-Serpent', where the idea of God is evoked as a tangible absence: 'It fits the universe man can ken / As a man's soul fits his body' – a Leviathan flickering round 'the cantles o' space' – everywhere present, nowhere to be seen. 'I feel like a star on a starry nicht, / A'e note in a symphony' MacDiarmid says, but he senses the whole starry night, the whole symphony surrounding him, animated – 'the serpent is movin' still'. Maybe 'the hert o' a man' feeling 'the twist in its quick' can 'raise a cry that'll fetch God back' – or perhaps the serpent is dying, like Christ, wounded in the side, the spirit ebbing like a tide, leaving bright but lonely pools behind. The poem ends attempting that cry of hope: 'Loup again in His brain, O Nerve', like a trumpet-call, clear as lightning on chaos, burning with 'the instant pooer / O' an only plan!' But the silence that surrounds the call continues after it.

Atheism, Nietzsche argued, might free mankind from 'this whole feeling of guilty indebtedness toward its origin, its *causa prima*. Atheism and a kind of *second innocence* belong together.' But the myth of the heroically isolated individual is also part of the idolisation of 'great men' and MacDiarmid seems to have accepted the Nietzschean image of the hero as outsider, opposed to and misunderstood by the majority who are always wrong. Nietzsche saw the increasingly democratic nature of society as the central social phenomenon of his era: the spreading disease of slave morality.

Nietzsche's analyses of the complementary roles of master and slave and their psychological effects clearly prefigure MacDiarmid's perception of the relation between Scotland and England, and the means by which Scotland might be culturally imagined out of a subject psychology. Since Christianity endorsed the master/slave dichotomy, MacDiarmid's unremitting atheism is a political argument attacking quiescence and surrender, self-righteous vanity or what the English poet John Milton called 'injured merit' – passivity was never a virtue for MacDiarmid. The notion of an omnipotent God (or metaphorically, an Anglocentric cultural and economic supremacy based in London) seemed poisonous to MacDiarmid. His struggle to find 'equal terms' in which to address 'God' or 'great men' in his poetry (Lenin, for example) is not simply a pathological flaw but a strategy in the struggle.

To MacDiarmid's generation, which saw the big words (like 'patriotism' and 'loyalty') killed off in World War I, the ruin of Europe made Nietzsche's radical rejection of bourgeois values dreadfully attractive and an international range of writers were keen to affirm the pre-eminence of the artist-creator-redeemer, an individual superior to the collective mass. In *A Drunk Man Looks at the Thistle* there are dozens of examples of imagery and thought which seem directly derived from Nietzsche's *Thus Spoke Zarathustra*, including the Great Wheel of the Cosmic Year, the crown of roses and the poem's essential trope of drunkenness. Compare MacDiarmid's 'There's nocht sae sober as a man blin' drunk' with Nietzsche's 'How it speaks soberly, this intoxicated poet!' or MacDiarmid's 'This munelicht's fell like whisky noo I see't' with Nietzsche's 'Does the moon not intoxicate us?' Perhaps even the parodic form of the *Drunk Man*, lurching from ribald 'sclatrie' (scandalous obscenities) to lyric perfection, from brutal anger to exquisite nuance, combining satire and philosophy, derives from Nietzsche.

Like Nietzsche, MacDiarmid goes to extremes and studies what happens there. In the 'Ode to All Rebels' (pp.194–6), his persona recollects feelings of carnal desire returning to him after the death of his first wife, even at the moment of her burial, shocking his sense of love's 'tender ties' in the reawakening of 'rude bluid'. Conventional pieties are luridly exposed. The poet then declares his preference for 'cruelty and lust and filth' over the hypocrisy of bourgeois towns in which each day unthinkable horrors take place: 'I am the woman in cancer's toils, / The man without a face.' He scorns all citizens and citizenship in the belief that

> There is nae horror history's ever kent
>   Mob passion or greedy fear wadna soon
> Mak' them dae owre again ...

and in a shuddering, unsettling refrain he excludes himself from the normal assumptions of social well-being:

> You may thank God for good health
>   And be proud to be pure
> In body and mind – unlike some.
> I am not so sure.

> You may feel certain that God
>   Is on the side of the sane
> And prefers your condition to syphilis.
> I am not so sure.

Congratulate yourselves you're spared
The ghastly ills others endure.
God's with the majority surely.
I am not so sure ...

In 'To hell wi' happiness!' (p.137), from *To Circumjack Cencrastus*, he seems set upon 'the terrifying discipline / O' the free mind' committed to taking a route far removed from the familiar lights of humanity. This extremism is more than a mere posture: MacDiarmid's life is proof of his commitment. His poetry is evidence of its integrity.

MacDiarmid and Modern Scottish Literature: Rediscovering National Traditions

When Hugh MacDiarmid began writing, Scottish literature was hard to find. There were few books about it and hardly any primary texts available besides the works of Burns and Scott. Why?

In 1603, after the death of Queen Elizabeth I (of England), King James VI (of Scotland) rode down to London with his courtiers and became James I (of an abruptly United Kingdom). This was the first defining moment in modern Scottish history, the transition from Elizabethan to Jacobean periods, from late medieval to early modern times.

In 1707, the Scottish Parliament signed itself and the nation's statehood out of existence and representatives of the Scottish people went to Westminster. The people themselves weren't asked but they protested about it. The Jacobite rising of 1745 led by Prince Charles Edward Stuart or 'Bonnie Prince Charlie' has been systematically wrapped in romantic glamour, but at the time it was a real threat to social and economic stability in Britain. The value of the British pound dropped to sixpence. After their defeat at Culloden in 1746, reprisals against Scottish Highlanders were brutal. The music, clothes and language of the Highlanders were outlawed: their culture was suppressed.

The prosperity of Edinburgh in the later eighteenth century coincided with poverty in the Highlands and elsewhere; Burns's *Poems* (1786) was immensely popular partly because it appealed across all social strata. To the sophisticated bourgeois, Burns was a miracle of nature, an inspired ploughman-poet; to the peasant and the poor, Burns's songs were immediately memorable, sung for pleasure.

Meanwhile, the vogue among the book-buying public was turning to long narrative poetry and in the early 1800s, Byron was the star. Walter Scott began in a similar way with *The Lay of the Last Minstrel* (1805). The archetypal Romantic declaration identifying self and land is nowhere more resolutely asserted:

> Breathes there the man, with soul so dead,
> Who never to himself hath said,
> This is my own, my native land!

But Scott then began writing novels, beginning with *Waverley* (1814), which fictionalised the 1745 Jacobite rising and mythologised it. Its subtitle, *'Tis Sixty Years Since*, implied that time enough had passed for the event to be thought of in a mood of romantic nostalgia. Scott also encouraged the reigning British monarch King George IV to visit Edinburgh in 1822 and to wear the kilt (though self-consciously the king chose to clothe his legs in pink tights): thus Highland Scottish culture was safely integrated as a component part of British identity. Highland military regiments might pride themselves in their Scottishness, but their military identity was ultimately British, and their service was finally to Victoria's Empire.

Scott's novels were internationally popular: read throughout Europe and Russia, they made Scotland a major destination on the tourist trail. In the United States, Mark Twain blamed Scott for the American Civil War because, he alleged, Scott's portrayal of chivalrous knights and gracious ladies in a firmly hierarchic social order was so attractive to Americans of the Southern States that they went to war to uphold such values (and to keep their slaves).

What was their effect in Scotland?

Throughout the nineteenth century, popular Scottish literature became increasingly incapable of dealing with growing industrialism or the conditions of the Highlands. As a direct result of the Highland Clearances from about 1814 on, the vast diaspora of Scots around the world was a ready market for nostalgic images and stories of a home they'd never return to. By the end of the century, a series of poetry anthologies known as the 'Whistle-Binkies' was providing sentimental verses derived from Burns's love songs but lacking Burns's poignant charm, subtlety and flair, while in prose the predominant school was that of the 'Kailyard' or vegetable garden: home-grown tales of small-town Scottish life with patronising wisdom dispensed by the local minister. The romance novels of Annie S. Swan and the Celtic twilight stories of Neil Munro were essentially escapist fiction for readers at home and abroad. S.R. Crockett, writing sweet stories like *The Lilac Sunbonnet* or boys' adventures like *The Raiders* and *The Men of the Moss Hags*, derived his vision of heroic deeds and domestic fidelities from a dull-witted acceptance of Scott's vision of his native land.

There was another side to the end of the nineteenth century, though. The poetry of John Davidson and James 'B.V.' Thomson revealed darker aspects of the Victorian psyche, urban degradation, the industrialised city, a world of alienation and despair. 'Mankind has cast me out' begins Davidson's *Testament of a Man Forbid,* and the haunting, nocturnal vision of Thomson's *City of Dreadful Night* has none of the 'Kailyard' pieties. MacDiarmid's poem 'Of John Davidson' (p.166) brings together individual loneliness and the universe of religious scepticism characteristic of the end of the nineteenth century: Davidson's suicide by drowning is remembered as 'A bullet-hole through a great scene's beauty, / God through the wrong end of a telescope'.

In novels, the other side of small-town Scotland was exposed by the appalling psychological oppression and physical violence depicted in the brutal tragedies of George Douglas Brown's *The House with the Green Shutters* and John Macdougall Hay's *Gillespie*. And while R.L. Stevenson was safely identified as a children's writer in *Treasure Island* and *Kidnapped*, he is more accurately a writer of childhood's end, as Jim Hawkins and David Balfour learn how to say goodbye to their colourful heroic mentors Long John Silver and Alan Breck Stewart, and *Dr Jekyll and Mr Hyde* is an unremittingly adult fable, the 'most serious' work, in Henry James's words.

But the world of Scottish literature in 1922 was aptly caricatured by MacDiarmid himself: like all other literatures, he said, it had been *written* 'almost exclusively by blasphemers, immoralists, dipsomaniacs, and madmen' – but, unlike most other literatures, it had been *written about* 'almost exclusively by ministers' – with the consequence that critical opinion had been neutralised.

So MacDiarmid's commitment was not only to writing poetry but also to revitalising the national cultural and literary climate in what he called 'a propaganda of ideas'. He set about this by writing a vast number of articles for newspapers and literary journals throughout Scotland and in London, and by publishing anthologies of contemporary Scottish poetry. One set of articles comprises 'A Theory of Scots Letters' (1923) in which the Scots language was considered not as a pawky vernacular idiom for small-minded canniness and sentimentality but, somewhat hyperbolically, as 'the only language in Western Europe instinct with ... uncanny spiritual and pathological perceptions'. Another series of articles, collected as *Contemporary Scottish Studies* (1926), began to establish the reputations of younger and more innovative writers, while demolishing those of their elders; similarly the series of three *Northern Numbers* anthologies began by including famous authors like John Buchan but then rapidly introduced poets with a sharper contemporary edge, and the third of the series seems to have deliberately included a larger proportion of women. Triply marginalised (as writers, as women, and as Scots), MacDiarmid recognised in such poets the potential for literary expression of a range of experience conventional writing hardly suspected, and he encouraged it. That aspect of his legacy has been of more benefit in the long term. Among his immediate contemporaries, the major Scottish writers of the 1920s and 1930s with whom MacDiarmid shared close creative friendships were all men – Compton Mackenzie (1883–1974), Edwin Muir (1887–1959), Neil Gunn (1891–1973), William Soutar (1898–1943), Lewis Grassic Gibbon (1901–35), Fionn MacColla (1906–75), as well as the artist William Johnstone (1897–1981) and the composer F.G. Scott (1880–1958). So were the group of poets who, across more than one generation, developed their art in MacDiarmid's company, and who knew him, to a greater or lesser degree of intimacy, as a friend: Robert Garioch (1909–81), Norman MacCaig (1910–96), Sorley MacLean (1911–96), Sydney Goodsir Smith (1915–75), George Mackay Brown (1921–96), Iain Crichton Smith (1928–98) and Edwin Morgan (b.1920). These writers collectively comprise the poetic *geist* of twentieth-century Scottish literature after MacDiarmid's cultural revolution of the 1920s and alongside MacDiarmid's later career.

Central to that *geist* was the gravitational pull of Scotland as the ground in which literary and intellectual work could be earthed, and an opposition (often voiced, almost always implied) to Anglocentrism. However, in 1936, in *Scott and Scotland*, Edwin Muir argued against separate Scottish traditions in the modern world: 'Scotland can only create a national literature by writing in English', Muir said. To MacDiarmid, this was a betrayal of all he had achieved and hoped to do, a strangling of literary possibility and an obsequious surrender to English authority. MacDiarmid spurned Muir's friendship and alliance, and scorned his conclusions.

Culturally, MacDiarmid won this battle. He fought for the development of a multivalent, multivocal literature whose coherence could be conferred by a specific but non-prescriptive national identity, which could be evaluated in an international context. In many respects this has happened. Having established Scots as a medium for serious literary expression in the 1920s, MacDiarmid increasingly insisted on the value of Gaelic language and culture in the 1930s, and the significance of the Celtic identity shared in the literatures of Scotland, Ireland and Wales. His hopes were answered in the publication of Sorley MacLean's first book of poetry *Dàin do Eimhir* in 1943, a crucial moment in the development of modern Gaelic literature. In the meantime, his own poetry had moved from using Scots as a predominant idiom to relying on a distinctly Scottish form of English, and introducing words and phrases from as many of the world's languages as could be tapped. This wasn't abandoning Scots but embracing the phenomenal twentieth-century possibility of global communication.

Since the 1960s, Edwin Morgan has furthered MacDiarmid's aspirations, in the diversity of his own poetry, in his use of both Scots and English, and in his translations from a range of languages. Like MacDiarmid, Morgan is an internationalist – but always with the double focus of what people have in common *and* what makes them so various. For Morgan, marginalisation becomes a matter for immediate revaluation. In his presence, sometimes under his tutelage, another wave of writers has appeared, whose different languages, experiences, motives and desires have been encouraged by the celebration of variety in all Morgan's work. In modern Scottish literature, the strongest drive towards that expressiveness began with Hugh MacDiarmid.

Critical Readings

1. Wonder and Mystery, Love and Death

MacDiarmid's poetry frequently raises the big questions. Because he asks them so vividly, so much in a spirit of wonder at creation's inexplicable magnificence, and so much with the sense of vulnerable human worth as a measure of value, he keeps them edged. No easy answers are allowed.

Wonder characterises 'Poetry and Science' (pp.228–9), where the 'rarity and value of scientific knowledge' is praised because it can 'Replace a stupefied sense of wonder / With something more wonderful / Because ... understandable'. He demonstrates this kind of understanding in such poems as 'Bracken Hills in Autumn' (pp.167–8), which is not only rich in colour and sensuality but is also analytic, describing what happens if cartloads of bracken are tipped into a pool where there are few fish: the 'swarming animalcula upon them / Will proportionately increase the fishes too'.

He is a poet of mystery in 'Harry Semen' (pp.191–2), which grimly asks the question what were the odds against the single seed, from which 'in sheer irrelevance I cam [came]'; he's a playful, delighted and marvellously eloquent poet in such bravura works as 'Water Music' (pp.153–6), an onomatopoeic depiction of the three rivers which come together in Langholm, the village where he grew up: the Wauchope, the Esk and the Ewes (as a boy, he fancied he could distinguish between them by sound alone). There is a freshness, a childish naïveté in some of MacDiarmid's work which is linked to adult compassion and mature wisdom. This is what happens in 'With the Herring Fishers' (pp.188–9), where the fishermen crying out to their catch to 'come walkin' on board' sound like God hauling in nets full of people:

> 'Left, right – O come in and see me,'
> Reid and yellow and black and white
> Toddlin' up into Heaven thegither ...

But these senses of mystery and wonder are complex keys to deeper issues. For Freud, human progress and mastery over nature was achieved at the cost of suppressing instinctual desires; consequently, not only individuals but whole civilisations might be neurotic. In the immediate aftermath of the 1914–18 war, this was horribly understandable. 'Prelude to Moon Music' from 'Au Clair de la Lune' (pp.11–13) begins: 'Earth's littered wi' larochs [ruins] o' Empires, / Muckle nations are dust ...' but the vast historical perspective dwindles quickly to an individual imagination, seen like Schoenberg's *Pierrot Lunaire*, in the shifting warp of moonlight:

> An' the roarin' o' oceans noo'
> Is peerieweerie to me:
> Thunner's a tinklin' bell ...

This dark unconscious world for MacDiarmid as for Freud is a multifaceted store of unutilised memories always simultaneously present.

Modern art (particularly that of Braque, Picasso and the Cubists) employs this sense of coexisting versions of different perspectives upon the same event. Simultaneity is brilliantly compressed in MacDiarmid's early poem 'The Universal Man':

> Helen's white breasts are leaping yet,
> The blood still drips from Jesus' feet,
> All ecstasies and agonies
> Within me meet.

The poet is all things, imagining all sides, Christian and pagan, 'in a thousand shapes'; he is 'what every newsboy shouts / And what God thinks'. He is the martyred Christ and his murderers, but also Aphrodite, ancient Greek goddess of love, and Eurydice, 'drawn from Hell' each year, like the returning spring; he is both man and woman, both earthly and divine.

One of the most arresting qualities of the early Scots lyrics is their universal viewpoint, as if all history and all cosmic space could be thought of and engaged. 'The Bonnie Broukit Bairn' (p.9) presents the earth as a poor, neglected child whose dirty hands rubbing tear-stained cheeks have left them streaked and grubby, surrounded by the adult grandeur, pomp and pretentiousness of Mars, Venus and the moon. The attractive personification belies the strength with which humane concern is directed towards unwarranted suffering. Beside the children of the earth, the astronomical universe is indifferent and irrelevent.

If 'The Bonnie Broukit Bairn' brings the cosmos to account in terms of human value, 'Empty Vessel' (p.19) effects a similar fusion of particular hurt humanity and the vastness of the universe, sweeping outwards from an encounter in a lonely countryside, where a young woman's tragic song of loss for an absent child seems an expression unequalled by anything in the world or even beyond it, in the music of the spheres.

MacDiarmid has sometimes been accused of inhumanity and a lack of warmth, but while these poems reject sentimentalism and withhold the consolations of religious belief, they are charged with resolute compassion.

The cosmic context and the distinction of human pathos within it is the keynote of 'The Dying Earth'.

'The Dying Earth' (p.8)

The title gives you the image: this poem is a vision of apocalypse, the end of the world. All the possibilities, all the things that might have happened, are being cancelled. Note how the verb works: 'Dying'. This is something that is happening now. It's not a vision of something that has happened and is over and done with; nor is it a prophecy of something that is going to happen one day. It's something continually happening, a process of changing, of becoming, or transforming, depicted in the poem itself.

It opens in pitch-black darkness, universal night-time: the day has gone, and with it the sunlight. God is still awake, though, even at this time of night, and his glances flash like lightning over the old earth as it dies. The second stanza opens by repeating the first phrase of the first stanza, as if to put a double layer of black paint on the canvas. Now God begins to speak, but not in commandments to others, only in broken or fragmented sounds, thunders, reminding himself of all that he had intended and hoped the world might have been, and how his plans had all gone wrong. God isn't described or depicted in human terms but he does behave in recognisably human ways: he is awake, tired, he glances and looks, he speaks, tells stories to himself.

In the third stanza, the element of pathos suggested in the best hopes and plans all wrecked is paramount: he cannot close his eyes, or turn away and rest, but is drawn back to look again and again, in glances that fly from pole to pole – cosmic lightning flashing from one end of the world to another – and his tears come down as he weeps in sorrow for all the tragedies and losses, the unfulfilled lives of individuals, communities, nations, like torrential bursts of rain, falling over everything.

The images of storm in the poem follow the natural sequence: lightning (1.2), followed by thunder (1.6), then the downpour (1.12). The image of dense darkness is unnatural, in the sense that this is a global dark, there is no day anywhere. God is referred to as 'he' but his human responses find expression in elemental forces. He's never described as an old man with white hair and a beard.

His eyelids are 'weary', but weary with exhaustion from frustrated hope, rather than age. The God of this poem has wished the earth might have become a better place, and cannot help looking desperately for some sign that it has, even as it reaches its end. All that is left to him is a wordless expression of sorrow for the waste.

It's a dense little poem, full of rich words and onomatopoeic sounds. The thick sounds of the repeated opening phrase, in stanzas one and two, deepen the darkness. The unpredictable rumbling of thunder is given in line 6; and you can hear the rainclouds unleashing themselves in the last line. The close-packed Scots vocabulary makes the sound and look of the words strange to the ear and unfamiliar on the page. By contrast, the metre and rhyme-scheme is straightforward: three stanzas of four lines each, each consisting of two rhyming couplets: AABB// CCDD//EEFF. But the rhymes and movement of the verse are always shifting. The longer syllables of 'God's waukrife yet' are a contrast to the quicker sounds of 'his glances flit' – as if to suggest the effort of weary wakefulness, as against the nervous and energetic 'glances'. And what God 'meent the warl' to be' has a wishful rightness to its sound that contrasts with the next line, as the plan 'gaed jee'. So while the metre is regular (each stanza structured on three four-stressed lines and a final three-stressed line), there's no sense of simple or merely pedantic repetition in the verse. The urgency and the sorrow in the tone combine, as the poem focuses on a barren or unconsummated world: what might have been becomes what never happened. Yet the symbol of rain is traditionally associated with regeneration, bringing life back to an arid world. If the earth is dissolved and destroyed in the wash at the end of the poem, it's only by such destruction that a fresh start might be made. But nothing in the poem points forward to that. There is no indication that this God will care again for a world: this world has taken all his hopes.

If 'God' is the ultimate abstraction, MacDiarmid brings material realities to bear upon and humanise 'Him' here. In 'Scunner' those realities are physical, the abstraction the ultimate ideal: 'Love'.

'Scunner' (p.18)

'Scunner' is an imaginary monologue, the interior voice of a man watching his lover rise from him and clothe herself after they have made love. The physical act of sex, the coupling, has just taken place, and each body is single again. The poem is about

something essential to any sexual human relationship: the
relation between physical action and idealising beauty. It's also a
comic poem, of generous sympathy and warm humour, tolerant
and wry, affirming in a shy afterglow. And it is an unsentimental
poem, shocking perhaps in the overt sexuality of its subject,
delicate in its balancing of language and tone, but firm in its
statement of preference.

The graceful movement of the body is, in the opening lines,
what hides the body itself: the physical presence is made into
something more than merely physical by virtue of the 'graces' in
which it hides or 'derns'. These 'graces' belong to the body, but
they're also perceived and enjoyed by the watcher: he recognises
their beauty. But he is under no illusion. In the same way, the
dull, ordinary earth hides itself under a field of golden grain. Out
of the death of pride – after carnal sexuality – 'you rise' and still
possess 'beauty' as a half-disguise. It's only half a disguise
because both parties have just experienced the death of pride –
shamelessness – and if beauty is in the eye of the beholder, this
beholder is about to recognise the particular quality of beauty he
is witnessing.

The outdoor reference to golden grain suggests a farming,
rural or pastoral context, but the second stanza begins with a
great leap in imagination: the twinkling stars are only dirt too,
seen from a distance. His gaze has rolled to the sky, then returns
to her once again: although you are far too close to me you are
still, sometimes, just like those distant stars, clothed in that same
beautiful light. Because we've been so close, I should see past the
beauty and recognise the creatural fact: that beauty is something
you should have lost. But it's there, a beneficent light. 'And I lo'e
Love / Wi' a scunner in't'.

'Scunner' is a traditional Scots word which is still commonly
spoken, though often self-consciously. In the 1920s, when
MacDiarmid wrote this poem, it was a word much more forcefully
signalling disgust and repulsion. MacDiarmid talks elsewhere of
the need to 'relish the element of degradation' and something of
that paradoxical necessity is present here. The distance between
spiritual love and carnal desire or base and brute animal lusts
and high intellectual pursuits is a Victorian convention and a
popular cliché, but here MacDiarmid is bringing grace and beauty
together with 'the death of pride' in an effortless insistence that
they should be understood and experienced together. Ideal 'Love'
with its capital 'L' and physical repulsion, the 'scunner', belong
with each other – but you have to recognise their distinction as

well as the intimacy of their identity. Like lovers, they are separate, but they are also united.

The tone is gentle, the transformation in the opening lines is wondrous and mysterious. But it isn't exaggerated or melodramatic: beautifully poised, the short lines are emotionally full of giving, but never gush. A wry humour enters the second stanza. Lines 9 and 10 are a single blunt, reductive sentence. One might have expected 'The skinklan' stars' to lead on to a more conventional romantic image of radiance, but line 10 knocks away such illusion, alliteration emphasising the point: 'Are but distant dirt.' The syntax qualifies the next statement: 'Tho' ... / ... still – whiles —' ('Although ... / ... nevertheless – sometimes —'), then the qualifications disappear and the affirmation comes, of carnal love brought together with romantic and spiritual love, relativising, enhancing and enriching each other.

The bringing together of 'contrarieties' has often been considered a curious property of Scottish literature since the scholarly critic G. Gregory Smith coined the phrase 'Caledonian antisyzygy' in 1919, in his book *Scottish Literature: Character and Influence*, arguing that the ability to move quickly from the respectable to the disreputable, to acknowledge 'the absolute propriety of a gargoyle's grinning at the elbow of a kneeling saint!' was essential to Scottish literature and life. The tendency to make sudden transitions between things or kinds of experience normally thought of as conflicting or distinct Smith considered the key to the Scottish character. Curiously enough, it is also a predominant characteristic of modern art and as we've noted, MacDiarmid was uniquely located to maximise the modernist literary potential in Scots – nowhere more extensively than in *A Drunk Man Looks at the Thistle*.

A Drunk Man Looks at the Thistle (pp.24–113)
The title is ironic. When the poem was published in 1926 a number of books or newspaper articles were ostentatiously using similar titles: 'An American Looks at His World' or 'An Irishman Looks at His World' for example. Such titles announced their own importance: they promised to provide a searching enquiry into a significant subject. But a drunk man looking at a thistle? It's a comic, ridiculous, self-deflating, rather unattractive prospect. MacDiarmid's intention was to undermine the complacent self-importance and pomp of his contemporaries and to reach deeper, into areas of understanding other than the scientific and analytical. The title already implies a sense of parody.

The first question is, 'What's it about?'

The first answer might be 'Scotland'. The poem is a meditation, a satire and an exposé of what 'Scotland' means (or meant in the 1920s). But it's also about identity. The poem has a double focus: a particular national identity and identity as such, what makes an individual. MacDiarmid is explicit about the gender of this individual: it is a masculine identity he's concerned to explore.

This twofold subject is announced in the title: a man, but in a peculiarly fluid and unfixed condition, and the symbol of Scotland. The question of national identity runs through the poem, but it's only one aspect of what constitutes the identity of the individual. Others, for example, include sexual (as we've noted), linguistic (Scots, not English), political (socialist, not conservative), social (working class), religious (unorthodox), and spiritual (yearning, often agitated, rather than tranquil).

Connected in the symbol of the thistle are other themes and subjects. There is the recurring concern with the terrific potential in human beings to do better, to become more fully human and to lead lives worth living, alongside the tragic sense of waste, the profligate squandering of worth to be seen in social organisation as in nature. There is the unanswerable opposition between volition and destiny, the will to move things into a different configuration and the inevitability of failure, how things fall back into an apparently preordained pattern. This can occur in personal, social or political spheres, both national and international. And there is the mystery of sexual identity, which returns in the poem again and again, sometimes celebrated, but more often the cause of anguished psychological self-questioning.

An explicit narrative frame is suggested by the title and the clues to a 'story' in the poem itself, but it would be dangerous to read these too literally. We are meant to imagine the man returning from a village pub where he's been drinking with his cronies, farm workers, Cruivie and Gilsanquhar; he's on his way home to his wife Jean. He stumbles by the roadside and in lines 96 and 104 describes himself as sprawled beneath the moon on a hillside surrounded by thistles and bracken. One particularly big thistle seems to rise up between him and the moon. He suffers from hiccups (l.233, 235, 237), maybe even vomits (l.1571), but eventually he's going to get home to his wife, and he predicts her response to his wayward wanderings in the last lines of the poem.

This theatrical reading isn't much help, though. The drama so conspicuously missing from this scenario is supplied to some extent by the play of images: the drunk man himself, the thistle and the rose, whisky and moonlight, the sea-serpent and woman (both his wife Jean and the idealised figure of the 'silken' lady).

But the symbols and images shift their shapes in the dance. Let's examine a passage from the poem in detail now, for a sense of that electrifying movement.

from A Drunk Man Looks at the Thistle: 'O Wha's the Bride' (ll.604–35, p.47)

A Drunk Man Looks at the Thistle relies on a stanza-form and metre closely related to the traditional Scottish ballad and many ballads frequently involve themes of dark mystery, linking sex and death. This, the most famous part of the whole work, distils and concentrates these themes.

A glance at the page shows you two different typefaces: the verses open with an address made by a man to a woman, and there are three passages in italics, each preceded by a long dash. These are the woman's replies to the man. So this is an imaginary dialogue. We've encountered an interior monologue in 'Scunner'; now the woman's voice engages in response to the man's questions. Yet it isn't a dramatic or theatrical presentation: these are imaginary voices held in the medium of the poem. The dialogue makes one poem of two voices: separate and distinct, yet connected, responsive, interactive. This too is a form often found in the traditional Scots ballads.

If the opening of the poem parodically refers to national identity, this passage is an enquiry into sexual identity, and there is no parody here: the tone is earnest and painful. Anguish, self-pity and doubt, fear, hurt, guilt and cruelty are all involved.

The question of the relation between sexual desire and romantic love has been approached and considered in various ways in the passages immediately preceding this one. The 'drunk man' has referred to his wife Jean and their relationship has prompted an imaginary dialogue between 'body' and 'mind'. As with the poem 'Scunner', feelings of love and revulsion are mixed: '... the mair scunnersome the sicht / The mair for love and licht he's fain [desirous] ...' (ll.600–1). The direct address to the woman shifts the tone from monologue to potential dialogue, registered in the transition in reference to the woman, from 'wha' (or 'who'), in line 604, to 'you' ('your bonny een') in line 606:

O lass, wha see'est me	(604)
As I daur hardly see,	(605)
I marvel that your bonny een	(606)
Are as they hadna seen.	(607)

The abject truth of physical, animal being lurks beneath the ideals of self-respect. But this conclusion is scarcely uttered before the woman's voice breaks in: 'If you could get behind the light of my eyes – which blinds you to the reality – you'd see something even more disgusting than anything you could imagine.'

The man's voice resumes after this warning and the tone here is shadowy and strange. It's as if he's helplessly committed to asking these unanswerable questions, knowing that by doing so he will be risking an encounter with deep and painful mysteries. There is something of the oracle in these verses. Who is the bride carrying the bunch of snow-white thistles? Why is her bridegroom a cuckold, knowing nothing of what he should dread, and what will he discover on their wedding night? The man's voice offers an explanation that explains nothing: closer than husband, closer to her than her very self, someone who had no need of it has done this *'evil thing'* and taken her virginity. Who was he? How did he 'get in'?

One might imagine any number of variations on a tragic story here. The promised wife whose love for another makes the marriage false. The wronged husband. The jealous lover. The woman whose desire overtakes her chastity. But all these theatrical types and situations seem extraneous to the poem. The mysteriousness evoked here is part of the poet's purpose. If the reader is asking 'What does it mean?' so are the voices in the poem.

The woman responds: 'A man that died before I was born has done this evil thing.'

What does this mean? Is this a supernatural figure? A ghost or demon lover?

The man replies angrily: 'And he has left your purity to me, but it's as if it belonged to a corpse, for he has taken your spirit.' And she responds in a tone of consolation: 'No woman has ever had anything more to give her husband, since Time began.' So this is the essential condition of human being: the poem seems to be saying that any individual woman pledged in marriage must suffer these conditions, and any husband must accept them. The closing verses, lines 628–35, begin with great consoling words: the woman promises to give her kindness, her willing hands, her breasts, her limbs *'like willow wands'* (a deliberate echo of the ballad of 'The Twa Magicians': 'The lady stands in her bower door, / As straight as willow wand ...'). And on her lips as he kisses her, she promises, he'll pay no more attention to any of these questions, and as he buries his face in her hair, she says, he'll forget. But the word *'forget'* is a hard rhyme with the last word of the stanza, and the last two lines are a shocking reminder of the questions themselves:

> *And on my lips ye'll heed nae mair,*
> *And in my hair forget,*
> *The seed o' a' the men that in*
> *My virgin womb ha'e met ...*

What's evident here is that more than one man is referred to and the woman is herself unravished, virginal. But what does that tell us? And where are we left?

Let's concentrate for a moment simply on the words we've read, without the help of critics or reference to MacDiarmid's sources. The emotional intensity of the words suggests a real and passionate man and woman, not merely symbols. There is physical actuality here: real seed, real lips, hair, flesh and blood. There is also the woman's promise of love and loyalty, of the chance to turn away from and forget, even for a while, the anxious, urgent questions at the heart of the mystery of being.

Given this mix of actual and abstract, tangible and imagined, what answer can be given to the pedantic critical question of meaning?

This is a poem about the mystery of being human, what human identity is. More precisely, it's about sexual identity: what defines us as men or as women. The tone of wonder is mixed with the confusion: there are no easy answers. But if the concern of the passage is to do with sexual identity and the security of such identity, how far it can be relied upon, then the essential mystery (and what inspires the questions) must lie in the fact that sexual identity is paradoxical. A man is the product of a man and a woman; he is half woman. A woman is the product of a man and a woman; she is half man. The seed of all the men that meet in the 'virgin womb' of any young woman belonged to her father, grandfathers, great-grandfathers, and so on: many men who died before she was born. No husband is so singularly a man that he is the first man his wife will know, for 'closer to'r than hersel' is the flesh of her own body, the cells and synapse structures of her brain – half of which come from her fathers.

The passage leaves all the mysteries unexplained. The paradox perpetuates itself. No answers will dissolve the need to ask these questions again, in every generation. Whatever social form of marital relations law, the church and convention might sanction, these concerns will always be there to trouble us. The idea of virginity was more important in the 1920s, when definitions of masculinity and femininity were imperative and more rigorously enforced in law and religion. MacDiarmid's challenge to such conventional rules is radical, and permanent.

He offers, and demands, a more compassionate and subtle understanding of what the individual might be.

'Milkwort and Bog-Cotton' (p.153)

This is one of the most beautifully modulated love poems, carefully changing tone, cadence and pitch from line to line, as an exclamation of command gives way to a direct declaration and evocation of love; then in the second stanza, the prayer-like expression of hope gives way to a sense of realisation and mature understanding of what the objectification of beauty entails.

The Scots expression 'Cwa" is an abbreviation of 'Come away'. The poem opens with strange words and odd images: eyes like milkwort (referring to the wild flower with tiny, pale, bright blue petals) and hair like bog-cotton (with white tassels like cotton-wool). No conventional image of a woman is evoked, but a strange feminisation of the uncultivated moorland wilderness is happening, and, while the invitation to 'come away with me' could be taken literally as an address to a person, it must also be understood as applying to the sensible visualisation of the Scottish landscape, this particular piece of the earth, which the speaker says he loves, 'in this mood' best of all: 'Come away and live with me in my imagination wherever I go' might be one way to paraphrase the sentiment – but it is a real life together that is promised – a real landscape in a real mind.

The mood is established by the movement of the third line with its gentle, emphatic pausing on 'shy' and 'spirit' and the words which are a simile for this tentative feeling, 'laich' and 'wind' – a low wind, moving horizontally across the landscape, almost diffidently, but without faltering. There is a steady, progressive movement in the shifting vowel sounds of the second half of that line: 'like a laich wind moves ...' brought out perfectly in the musical setting of the poem by F.G. Scott.

No shadows can be cast from the sky across this landscape: it's a cloudless day and the eyes and hair of the beloved person – or the flowers of the moorland themselves – are seen clearly in uninterrupted sunlight. So the metaphor is working at a high level of sophistication. This is, undeniably, a love poem, but it's impossible to say whether a woman is symbolising Scotland or Scotland is being addressed as a woman. The objectification of love is what's crucial here. Perhaps the matter of national identity is not so important either, for despite the language of the poem, there is no assertion of Scottishness as such: this wilderness, in a sense, could be almost anywhere.

But this is not a poem in which the idealisation of the object will be allowed to dominate. It is a much tougher, wiser and more mature love that is finding expression here. The second stanza begins by noting that despite the beautiful, cloudless, shadowless day, in autumn the leaves will fall, and circling over each other as they do so, they will cast shadows themselves. If only that didn't have to happen! And if only roots didn't have to bury themselves in darkness under the earth, in order to allow such beauty as can be seen in these flowers to blossom! The sacrifice roots make to allow the expression of beauty is also inevitable, however. And deep surrounding darkness is always the price of light. The greater the dark, the greater the clarity in contrast to it.

The poem might have ended there with this traditional moral perception. But MacDiarmid brilliantly goes not one, but two, stages further. If only light revealed nothing 'but you' he says – and the implication is clear: sadly, the light does reveal all sorts of other things, not all of them so beautiful. And if only night concealed nothing else but the roots that allow such beauty to bloom – and the implication here is more sinister: night does conceal a great many other things too.

What survives in the poem, miraculously, given the darkness of what it's saying, is the feeling of love and the value of love, even at the price that is paid for it. The emphasis is firmly and gently placed upon the shy spirit moving to make its declaration of desire, the wish that light might reveal 'Naething but you'. In tonal modulations subtly blending regret and affirmation, wonder and resolve, the musical setting by F.G. Scott reproduced at the end of this book beautifully enhances this expression of love.

'Perfect' (p.210)

'Perfect' has been subjected to more scrutiny than most poems because of a spate of correspondence in the *Times Literary Supplement* in the 1960s.

It's still possible to find people who know nothing about MacDiarmid except that he plagiarised other people's writing. Almost every word in 'Perfect' has been sourced: the location given under the title, the Spanish epigraph and the words of most of the text come, respectively, from the Scottish authors Seton Gordon and R.B. Cunninghame Graham, and a short story by the

Welsh writer Glyn Jones. (All the sources are available in the
Penguin edition of the *Selected Poems*.)

The *TLS* correspondence flared up the accusation of plagiarism
when the words of the text of the poem were shown to have been
taken from Glyn Jones's story 'Porth-y-Rhyd'. MacDiarmid
himself had not read the story, apparently, but he'd seen a review
of the book in which it appeared, which quoted the relevant
extract, and he'd fastened onto the key phrases and lifted them
into a different idiom.

The meaning of the poem bears no relation to the story. The
poem, unlike the story, presents no characters, no social
relationships, no narrative. Instead it presents a delicate but
sharply focused image, and the image connects with the poem's
epigraph, location and title to effect a moment of strange
realisation, an implicit statement about the nature of mortality.
Perhaps it's surprising that the poem has come through such
prejudice and hostility and still reads hard, intact, flawless and
fresh, but you needn't be bothered by the controversy to get to
grips with the poem itself.

South Uist is one of the furthest islands out from the mainland
of Britain. You'll find it on a map north of Ireland, among the
Outer Hebrides. Its western seaboard is the furthest west you can
get before the ocean: the next land beyond it is America.

The Spanish epigraph means 'The dead open the eyes of those
who live.' But there's an ambiguity in the phrase; it could be read
another way, to mean 'The dead open *their* eyes *on* those who
live.' The sense plays back and forth ambiguously. This
traditional image of death (the skull is frequently seen as a
'memento mori' or reminder of your own mortality, in paintings)
speaks to the living.

The bird in the original short story is a seagull; in the poem it's
a pigeon. Why? The pigeon is a homing bird and the west is the
traditional location of the Gaelic 'land of the ever-young': heaven,
the final spiritual homeland. Is there a suggestion that the bird
was flying towards an ultimate home? The skull is discovered on
the very edge of the European archipelago and the ultimate
boundary of Scotland.

There is certainly a suggestion that the bird's flight was
determined and decided by the brain that 'fixed the tilt of the
wings'. The line-breaks and punctuation in the second stanza all
serve to emphasise patterns of alliteration (the rhyming of
consonant-sounds like the 'b' and 'k' sounds in 'back' and 'beak')
and assonance (the rhyming of vowel-sounds, like the 'ih' sound in

'fixed', 'tilt' and 'wings'). There is in this a clear insistence upon a determined network of connections.

But the poem doesn't explain or elaborate any of its implications. It presents an image of startling and constant clarity, 'perfect' in itself, that holds forth the ambiguity of mortality. Perfection is achieved only in death. The skull's delicate structure held and sustained a spirit and mind which gave it direction in life. The wings themselves and the bird in flight are only present in the poem as imaginary historical events, inferences one can draw from the hard fact of the skull. The skull itself is all presence.

The idea of perfection refers to this problem of movement and stasis. To be perfect is to be incapable of change, as perfection is by definition the highest attainable state: any change from it would blemish it, and true perfection cannot blemish itself. 'Perfect' doesn't explore this problem, although it suggests it; it simply holds forth an image. In Robert Frost's famous definition of a poem, 'Perfect' is 'a momentary stay against confusion'.

'Crystals like Blood' (p.263)

'Crystals like Blood' ends in a world very different from that in which it begins. It works by a series of imaginative switches, from one brightly lit picture to another; they are seemingly unrelated until the final verse-paragraph draws them all together in an unexpected revelation of what the poem has in fact been about all along. The last lines have a sort of retroactive effect, altering everything that precedes them. What we have just read becomes something else once we become aware of the metaphoric connections between the images and the subject the poem is dwelling upon.

The subject is death: the personal death of a loved one. He or she is never specified but the intensity of emotion suggests that this isn't only an elegy; it's also a declaration of loyalty.

The poem is in four paragraphs and three parts. It opens with a simple assertion: 'I remember how, long ago, I found / Crystals like blood in a broken stone.'

The image from the title is dazzling: bright, hard, a combination of mineral and animal essence, the blood congealed in light-glancing crystals. There is no hint of where the poem might go with this opening; there are various possibilities.

The second paragraph is a hard-focus description of this discovery: the geologist's vocabulary is specialised, yet it gives a vivid visual impression of what it might have felt like to hold the stone in your hand and turn it. Different senses are involved:

colour, texture and weight are evoked, each making the 'broken chunk of bed-rock' more physically imaginable. Particularly deft is the almost explanatory tone of 'It was heavier than one would have expected / From its size'. This will have another resonance later on, as a metaphor for something which might appear small but is actually full of meaning, but as we read the poem for the first time, the phrase applies directly to the chunk of stone.

Then there is an abrupt shift of location and imagery. Instead of a world of nature we're in a world of mechanical engineering and industry. The deceptive opening phrase, 'And I remember ...', seems disarming. Again, there is no hint of where the poem is taking us. The formula is repeated: the poem begins 'I remember how ...' and the second part begins 'And I remember how ...' and the final part begins 'So I remember how ...' The structure couldn't be more obvious.

The description of how mercury is extracted from cinnabar is dynamic but there still seems no overt involvement made by the speaker. These are strong memories, but no explanation is given yet as to why they should be meaningful, so a kind of mysterious tension is building up in the poem: the energy is palpable, yet suspended, as it approaches the final paragraph.

The first line of this paragraph is almost prosaic. There's no lyrical posturing in the ego that remembers 'how mercury is got' – those last two monosyllables are blunt – when he contrasts his

> living memory of you
> And your dear body rotting here in the clay
> — And feel once again released in me
> The bright torrents of felicity, naturalness, and faith
> My treadmill memory draws from you yet.

The revelation that all along the poem has been an elegy, from the perspective of an atheist and materialist whose commitment is absolute, has been made with a perfect sense of timing and poise. The brutality of material fact is there, along with the expression of tenderness, and it is these two senses (the brutal and the tender) coming together in the line 'And your dear body rotting here in the clay' which clasps the energies of the poem and resolves the suspense in the admission of direct address. The poem is now spoken to the dead beloved: it is not simply reminiscence, but a focused expression of conviction. The sense of release this affords is there in the movement of the penultimate line: 'The bright torrents of felicity, naturalness, and faith'. The poem won't end with this romantic, emotional gesture, however, but connects with the piledrivers of the second paragraph, referring to the speaker's memory as a 'treadmill' continuing to draw these qualities out of itself and the fact of the other person – now no more material than her or his buried carcass, but miraculously capable of continuing to generate these affirming energies, despite all else. In a way this too is a love poem, not morbid, but recognising in wonder and mystery the 'at least partly understood' ground of living hope.

2. Political Themes

It's impossible to overestimate the significance of the nationalist and socialist revolutionary movements that took place when MacDiarmid was a young man: the miners' strike and riots in South Wales which he covered as a reporter in 1911 ('It's like living on the top of a volcano down here,' he wrote); the Easter Rising in Ireland in 1916, the Irish Civil War and the establishment of the Irish Free State in 1922; the Russian Revolution in 1917; the 1919 strike in Glasgow and the threat of a 'Red Clyde'; the first Labour government in Westminster in 1924; the founding of the National Party of Wales in 1925 and the National Party of Scotland in 1928. MacDiarmid was in British Army uniform when news of the Easter Rising in Dublin broke out; in a late interview he said his first impulse had been to desert and join the Irish.

The early poem 'Cattle Show' (p.8) hints at political violence to come, describing a display of bulls and brood mares at a farmers' exposition then turning to the 'countesses' and 'painted ladies' whose costumes and make-up suggest a world of social pretension due to be undermined by the world of animal reality, both in sexual terms (the 'red faces and virile voices' of the men seem slightly threatening from the first line) and in class terms (the glittering 'summer lightning' in the last line suggests a coming storm).

'Cattle Show' works by implication. More explicit depiction of Marxist ideas is found in 'Frae Anither Window in Thrums' (pp.126–32) from the long poem *To Circumjack Cencrastus*. Here the poet presents himself in anti-Romantic light, a wage-slave, a newspaper reporter cursing the financial status of his editor, with

> ... his new hoose, his business, his cigar,
> His wireless set, and motor car
> Alsatian, gauntlet gloves, plus fours and wife,
> — A'thing included in his life;
> And, abune a', his herty laughter ...

MacDiarmid's voice merges with that of his persona as he deplores the economic condition he suffers under: 'Curse on the system that can gie / A coof like this control o' me'. His dark imagination turns in its frustration towards the 'coontless opportunities' creativity might make for itself.

As opposed to those creative opportunities, it's the commodity-fetishism of popular Scottish fiction which MacDiarmid despises in 'Hokum' (pp.132–4), counterpointing his poverty (as a poet committed to art and ideas) against the mass preference for 'hokum' (entrancing rubbish) in a style of writing that is itself pastiche doggerel, a kind of anti-hokum. The sing-song rhythms and forced rhyme castigate popular taste and its exploitation by the purveyors of hokum. Referring to the romanticised notion of the self-sacrificing Scottish soldier featured in music-hall songs and popular novels, MacDiarmid rejects the hokum and confirms hope:

> It isna fair to my wife and weans,
> It isna fair to mysel'.
> The day's lang by when Gaels gaed oot
> To battle and aye fell.
> I wish I was Harry Lauder,
> Will Fyffe or J.J. Bell,
> — Or Lauchlan Maclean Watt
> For the maitter o' that!
> — Dae I Hell!

This is an extreme rejection of popular entertainers and a declaration of commitment to a deeper sense of value, a more humane, less superficial world. MacDiarmid's 'Hymns to Lenin' are explorations of the furthest regions of that essentially humane commitment. His infamous question in the 'First Hymn' (pp.139–40) ('What does it matter whom we kill if we lessen the worse murder of capitalism, which deprives most people of real lives?') is wholly atrocious only if one stays with the shock of the first phrase; the desire to allow people the opportunity to get lives that are worth having is surely humane, and the rhetorical question is a courageous way of insisting upon the need to count the cost, and not be content with sentimental wishfulness. He won't let you forget that a price must be paid, but his belief in human possibility activates his deepest scorn for those people and regimes he felt were hostile to it.

In 'from "England's Double Knavery"' (pp.226–7), MacDiarmid viciously caricatures the Fascist poet Roy Campbell: 'poor opisthocoelian Campbell' and Campbell's 'typical reader':

> — A stout man, walking with a waddle, with a face
> Creased and puffed into a score
> Of unhealthy rolls and crevices
> And a red and bulbous nose ...
> ... a man whose fat finger
> Ticks off the feet in Campbell's lines
> 'Left, right! Left, right!'

But even here, MacDiarmid turns from denigration to an assertion of value. Having debunked Campbell ('The hero of a penny novelette / With the brain of a boy scout') and bluntly dismissed his warrior code ('All soldiers are fools. / That's why they kill each other') he sets against the commonplace 'deterioration of life under the regime / Of the soldier' the idea of cultural diversity:

> The effort of culture is towards greater differentiation
> Of perceptions and desires and values and ends,
> Holding them from moment to moment
> In a perpetually changing but stable equilibrium ...

For MacDiarmid, this is what peace should be about, the opposite of the 'animus of war' which enforces uniformity and extirpates 'whatever the soldier / Can neither understand nor utilise ...' 'At the Cenotaph' (p.197) ruthlessly attacks the sanctimonious pieties associated with imperialist war and in 'Another Epitaph on an Army of Mercenaries' (p.201) he passionately denies any heroism in the lives of 'professional murderers': 'In spite of all their kind some elements of worth / With difficulty persist here and there on earth.'

For MacDiarmid, politics was a passion. He attempts to bridge the seemingly impassable gulf between great art and factory workers in 'The Seamless Garment' (pp.141–4), imaginatively addressing a cousin at work in a mill, where the unfamiliar factory machinery is bewilderingly complex to the poet but easily comprehended by the worker: if these looms can turn out such renowned border cloth, he asks, 'Shall things o' mair consequence shame us?'

The Marxist insistence that social change might be brought about wilfully by the working class (because their labour literally creates society's wealth) was based upon a theoretical understanding of industrialised society. For Marx, capitalism was not the only economic structure an industrial society might be based upon and even a capitalist economy might be revolutionised very quickly. Writing about Britain, Marx and Engels pointed out that to understand the British Empire one had to understand Britain as an Empire in itself. The colonial subjugation of the people of Ireland and the Highlands of Scotland was one focus of their analysis. Another was the probable outcome of imperialism: world war.

One of the angriest of MacDiarmid's anti-war poems is 'In the Children's Hospital' (p.199), which takes the acidly ironic line by Siegfried Sassoon as an epigraph: 'Does it matter – losing your legs? ...' and pictures a legless boy in the children's ward, visited by a Princess, whose 'hand of Royalty' will pat his head ('such an honour') as he struggles to walk with crutches. The rage builds line by line in packed rhymes ('crutches' ends line 2, making the words 'such is' at the end of line 4 monosyllabic blocks, leading into the staccato decree at the beginning of line 5, 'The will of the Princess'). The rhymes build in intensity (ABCBDEFEGGHHII), ending with three boiling couplets. The loss of the boy's limbs is a tragedy made more awful by the sheer obscenity of the delicately condescending 'pat' on the head. The 'honour' bestowed and the jealousy of all the other children dreadfully mock the sanctimonious platitude 'it's been all for the best!' Then the final couplet breaks the dam of outrage and the lasting reproach of the curse is delivered in full volume: 'But would the sound of your sticks on the floor / Thundered in her skull for evermore!' The poem's vilification has lost none of its pertinence since it was published in 1935.

These political themes are explicit and strong in a number of MacDiarmid's poems, but they run implicitly through many others. Let's look at three which open up different political questions: one focused with angry intensity on Scotland and the tragedy of the Highland Clearances, one to do with the relation between exceptional individuals and the masses, and one embroiled in the turbulent world of early twentieth-century Europe.

'The Dead Liebknecht' (p.17)

Along with Rosa Luxemburg, Karl Liebknecht was the founder of the socialist group which was to become the German Communist Party – an extremely dangerous political force. Recognising its potential, Lenin was prepared to postpone the Russian socialist revolution if the German one came first. In the event, Liebknecht was arrested and executed; but by that time, the Russian Revolution was already underway.

The German poet Rudolf Leonhardt wrote this poem in the first place; it was translated into English and published in an anthology by Babette Deutsch and Avrahm Yarmolinsky (this version is reproduced at the end of this book); but in MacDiarmid's Scots version a chilling element of horror inhabits the exhilaration of the call to liberation. Liebknecht may have been a martyr to his cause, but the poem is double edged about the cost of such a cause, and this doubleness of vision runs right through it. The man is not turned into a glorious hero of the revolutionary movement – that would be a facile caricature. The poem is an attempt to understand the energies such action as Liebknecht's might unleash, and how they might take shape, as blessing or as curse.

The poem begins with an image of Liebknecht's corpse, lying above the city – any city – hovering, weightless, like a cloud or a vast World War I zeppelin, covering every square and every street in the urban map unrolled below. The martyr's blood spills from his wounds, running through the skies and casting shadows over all the houses and the people who inhabit them. The image of spilt blood filling the skies recalls a famous play by Christopher Marlowe, a contemporary of Shakespeare. In Marlowe's *Dr Faustus*, Faustus sells his soul to the Devil in exchange for knowledge and experience. When the time comes for Faustus to repay the bargain, he tries to get out of it and repents, calling on Christ his saviour to redeem him from the fires of Hell. In his final soliloquy, he says:

> The devil will come, and Faustus must be damned.
> O I'll leap up to my God! Who pulls me down?
> See, see, where Christ's blood streams in the firmament!
> One drop would save my soul ...

But not a drop is spared to save him, and Marlowe's Faustus meets his end. MacDiarmid's Liebknecht takes the role of Christ, a martyr dying to save others. But the working-class people in the city below seem overshadowed by his corpse; their houses are 'darkened' with his blood.

The second stanza takes us down into the city itself. From a fantastic vision, we're now in a world of horribly loud noise: factory horns blaring out over each other. This signals not an ordinary end to the working day but the dawn of socialism: the permanent revolution of the working-classes. The workers are let loose, and at first the idea of repressed energy suddenly released suggests an animal savagery. But then we are looking at the crowds and crowds of working people, moving in the streets like ants – scattering, everywhere becoming dispersed.

This is terrifically ambiguous. The sense of energy released goes with the sense of not knowing what will happen to it next. Shock at the magnitude of the moment brings not only wonder and amazement, but also terror.

The final couplet defines this ambiguity in a horrific image. From the skies, we've moved down to the city streets; now we go under the earth itself, to where Liebknecht's physical corpse is rotting in its grave. The white teeth of the skull are shining in a permanent smile: a beneficent smile of recognition? Or a macabre memento mori, a reminder not only of the death that comes to all individual men and women, but also to all political causes, however righteous or inspired, however evil or insane?

It's a poem that might make you shiver if you let it do that, recognising the force in the movement of people massed in social groups, and how helpless the individual is in such a context. Whether the smile of Liebknecht's corpse is approving or warning, the poem involves a hard recognition of the pathos of the epic effort.

'The Dead Liebknecht' was published in MacDiarmid's second collection of lyrics, *Penny Wheep*, in 1926. In 1921, the Irishman W.B. Yeats had published a poem about the armed military uprising in Dublin, called 'Easter 1916' in his book *Michael Robartes and the Dancer*. The Easter Rising was unpopular, but when the British sentenced its leaders to death, the executions turned them into martyrs and a great tide of popular feeling arose which fuelled Irish resistance to British rule, and led to the struggle for Irish independence, then the Irish Civil War, and eventually the establishment of the Republic. Yeats's poem commemorates the leaders who were shot and the cause in which their sacrifice was made, but it is not an unambiguous assertion of national identity. Rather, it is a painful recognition of the complexity of idealistic hopes and petrifying violence crystallised in the Easter Rising. The poem's refrain applies to the visionary moment of liberation that is also the focus of 'The Dead Liebknecht': everything is 'changed', Yeats says, 'changed utterly' – all has been 'Transformed utterly: / A terrible beauty is born'.

In both MacDiarmid's and Yeats's poems, there is the grim sense of what is 'terrible' and the sober understanding of what inspiring 'beauty' there is in the hope of liberation – either from the oppression of British colonialism in Ireland, or from the oppression brought about by industrial slavery in Liebknecht's Germany. In MacDiarmid's idiom, both nationalist and socialist ideals are reflected.

'On the Ocean Floor' (p.197)
This is a four-line poem with a pronounced rhyme: ABAB (where A is a weak, B a stronger rhyme), as if to suggest one layer folded upon another layer, each long line in itself like one geological stratum upon another. The tone is of quiet realisation, coming to an understanding of oneself gradually but forcefully, beginning to comprehend, then fully comprehending, a meaning, something in life that explains something about what life is.

The syntax works to create this mood with a relaxed yet tense beginning: 'Now more and more on my concern ...' (the word 'on' relates to the imagery of stratification and growth) '... my concern with the lifted waves of genius gaining ...' (the word 'genius' immediately introduces the romantic notion of the isolated artist, estranged from society, yet somehow also the only true judge of human worth): but what does the participle do? It ends the line, and so is emphatic and important, but it seems to relate to nothing in the line itself. What is 'gaining'? As we read the first line (it seems that 'my concern with ... genius' is what's gaining, but that's wrong) we feel that *something* is 'gaining' (superseding, overtaking, growing upon) increasingly ('Now'), so there is a quiet tension in the line. The second line supplies the answer: what's 'gaining' or becoming more important is the *awareness* of 'the lightless depths' that lie beneath these 'waves of genius'.

This is an image that swings two ways. It sets up a division between 'genius' and 'lightless depths' and the poem is about to occupy those 'depths' with 'foraminifera' – small crustacean animals whose dead bodies decay and whose shells accumulate, growing into great contours shaping the ocean floor and affecting the moving tides. This is a metaphor for the millions of working-class people whose lives have been and gone in history, while 'genius' is recorded as a lifting 'wave'. The division between 'genius' and 'foraminifera' is there, and the poem is élitist in that sense. But look at the subject of the poem: 'my concern'. It is a poem about a personal realisation of what is *relatively* important. The 'lifted waves' may be 'genius' but they are only waves – sea water, flashing, frothing, gone: an upsurge of power, turning to froth, into the air. There are beneath them unknown depths where other strengths amass, ignorant to 'genius' but actual ('their tiny shells' suggests a multitude of individual identities, whereas 'waves of genius' suggests undifferentiated creativity).

A semi-colon ends line 2. The odd phrasing that begins line 3 keeps the poem suspenseful. Syntactically, it could be paraphrased thus: 'Now more and more ... I am concerned with

[this]; ... And as one who hears [this].' In other words the grammatical suggestion of the phrase 'And as ...' would normally suggest a further clause ('And as one who hears [this, *I therefore feel this* ...]'); but that final clause doesn't arrive. Instead, we're left with the link back ('And as one who ...' refers to 'I am aware of ...') and the movement of the poem takes us forward to the final words. These offer no semantic resolution, but a beautifully effective image, in sound (this is what onomatopoeia is really all about) and visually. The tension is carefully maintained by the use of the word 'their' in the penultimate line: we do not know what it refers to until the last line, and the penultimate word, the one completely magical word in the poem: 'foraminifera'. The sighing assonance and alliteration in the last two lines is beautiful ('n' and 'sh'/'ss' in 'tiny shells incessantly raining' and 'f', 'o' and 'r' in 'On the ocean floor as the foraminifera die.').

This is an enormously compassionate statement, the statement of a spectator of all his own limitations. Try it out in your own voice; the sound you make is part of its meaning.

'The Glen of Silence' (p.209)

The depopulation of the Scottish Highlands in the early nineteenth century, the 'Highland Clearances', is arguably the central tragic event of modern Scottish history, similar in importance to the Great Famine in Irish history. In Calum MacLean's words: 'The initial causes were violent and completely criminal. The continuance of that depopulation ought to be a very heavy weight on the conscience of any civilised government.'

As well as bearing on our understanding of historical events, the images and symbols of the Highland Clearances have a lasting significance in novels such as Neil Gunn's *Butcher's Broom* (1934), Fionn MacColla's *And the Cock Crew* (1945) and Iain Crichton Smith's *Consider the Lilies* (1968). And it's worth looking at Tom Faed's 1865 painting 'The Last of the Clan' (in the Glasgow Kelvingrove Art Gallery and Museum) to get a sense of the 'golden glow' of sentimental Victorian solemnity in which the events were seen. By contrast, William McTaggart's proto-impressionist masterpiece 'The Sailing of the Emigrant Ship' of 1895 (National Gallery of Scotland, Edinburgh) is cold: blues, greys, greens, the distant ship on a horizon bisecting the canvas, the figures on the foreshore almost invisible, as if ghostly presences, sketched in, a woman in a white bonnet, a man with a shepherd's crook, a younger woman with a baby, and a dog with its long face pointing exactly in the direction of the departing vessel. The desolation of the scene is caught in the empty sky, not tranquil but turbulent, with a fragment of rainbow and huge billowing clouds. In the right foreground, four boats are drawn up. The absence of men is eerie. The painting evokes the silence of irredeemable loss.

This tragic sense is even more fully explored in more recent work, such as John Bellany's 'The Obsession' (1968; City of Edinburgh Art Centre) or the work of Will Maclean, like 'Skye Fisherman: In Memoriam' (1989; Dundee Art Galleries and Museums) in which particular individuals and occupations are seen in the context of economic realities, in a universe of spiritual uncertainty.

'The Glen of Silence' (1938) opens with an epigraph from the greatest of the ancient Greek tragedians, Aeschylus. A translation from the Greek is provided, but the strangeness of the Greek alphabet in the words upon the page has a twofold effect, emphasising the difference and distance of the original from ourselves and at the same time insisting on the contemporaneity of human tragedy. These events might have taken place long ago or in another country, but anyone at any time can know what these words mean. It's exactly this movement through the particular to universal recognitions that is essential to tragedy, and essential to the meaning of 'The Glen of Silence'.

Tragedy, as Adrian Poole has said, 'is a means of honouring the diversity of human beings, as individuals and in relation to each other and their world'. 'The menace and promise of tragedy' lie in the 'recognition of the sheer potentiality of all the selves we might be, and of all the worlds we might make together or destroy together.'

All these matters apply to 'The Glen of Silence': the context of Scottish history, which has left actual valleys and glens like Strathnaver in Sutherlandshire inexpressibly beautiful and utterly desolate, the historical extinction of cultures and languages, and the universal context of human tragedy are all implied by the poem. And in the poem's own terms the relation between individual and social worlds is acutely understood.

It opens in a curiously muted tone, with a reflective, self-directed question which runs over the first quatrain. The first line evokes an uncertainty between actual and imagined: quotation marks around the word 'heard' suggest that this audible silence is uncapturable, glimmering and accentuated by a solitary bird's 'cries' (the word is chosen not only for its rhyme but also in preference to 'song') and a 'brawling burn' (the image of futile struggle suggested there is carefully judged and unemphatic).

The stillness of tone is maintained in the second stanza, as the rhetorical question is answered. The 'stillness of foetal death' and the 'silence over the abdomen' are vivid and immediate images, yet they are metaphors for the stillness and silence the speaker – or the spectator, the reader's representative – perceives in the valley. The connection between the individual woman who has lost her child and the entire communities of people with a culture and language of their own, is metaphoric. But the metaphor is fearfully appropriate and 'foetal death' immediately becomes a symbol of social destruction. Again the word 'heard' is given in quotation marks but this time to emphasise its presence: it is a silence 'literally "heard"' – the oxymoron adds pressure to the language. So does the medical and clinical term 'auscultation' as its impersonality evokes the particular person in the specific intensity of her condition. The objectivity of the language heightens the passionate grief within it.

The last stanza is made up of five lines, ending in a one-line exclamation. At first glance the rhythm and shape of the poem suggest the structure of a traditional form but the curious rhyming ABCB, DECE, FGEHG and the fact that it terminates at line 13 make it an abruptly aborted sonnet. We are reminded of the sounds actually audible in the valley, echoing the first stanza in exactly the same tones: the bird's 'wheeple' is reminiscent of 'cries' (again, it's not 'song' and hints at despair, and it's a rhyming word) and the burn's 'bickering' (again, a futile struggle). Then comes the Gaelic phrase which links back to the epigraph, connecting the dead language of ancient Greece with the almost-exterminated language of modern Scotland: equally unpronounceable to most English-language readers the world over, and meaning *exactly the same thing*.

3. Visions of Hope: Nation and Identity

There's a marvellously chilling moment towards the end of Ibsen's great play *Peer Gynt*, where the Button-Moulder reminds Peer that he will die and all his exploits will be turned into eternal oblivion and all his ego will be returned to the mould. As if in glorious defiance of this, MacDiarmid's short comic masterpiece 'Crowdieknowe' (p.14) depicts the day of resurrection, literally, with men and women scrambling from the crowded earth to look up at God and his 'gang' of angels in the sky, to stare aggressively at them and ask who they think they are to stir them from their slumber.

The language of the poem is vigorous and robust, but it's also subtle. Consider the opening line: half serious (he'd really like to be there, it would be a sight worth seeing), half mock-romantic, distantly (and ironically) recalling Wordsworth's famous lines in *The Prelude* (1850 version, Book XI, ll.108–9) about the rise of the Romantic and revolutionary era: 'Bliss was it in that dawn to be alive, / But to be young was very Heaven!'

It isn't necessarily a Christian poem, though it describes an event promised by Christian myth, but devout Christianity was the atmosphere of MacDiarmid's domestic boyhood and there's a distinctly autobiographical timbre to it. The resurrected men are big, bearded, thundery, not at all peaceful: their character and nature is itself defiant, on the lookout. They're borderers. With them was always the sense that the enemy was just over the border. MacDiarmid's pride in this ancestry is evident: he might have wept in fear of them when he was a child, but who would not admire their stand against an omnipotent deity and his 'French-like' (fancily dressed, pontificating) attendants?

The women folk are more cautious, hesitantly seeking to make them 'haud their row' (restrain their blaspheming), worried about what might befall them at God's hand. But it is their unvanquished defiance in the face of ultimate opposition that MacDiarmid identifies with and celebrates.

Note how this spirit of defiant identity fuses *individual* characters (although no one is named), a *group* of people bound together by locality as well as a common condition, and what we might call the *national* character. Although MacDiarmid is careful not to elaborate analogies, it's an emblematic scene: David and Goliath, the little nation and the mighty empire, the Wild Bunch hopelessly outnumbered by the Mexican Army, law and order confronted by eternally rebellious, undefeated courage. If this comic resurrection is local and specific, it's also intended as an essentially Scottish stance (that's evident in the vernacular idiom of the Scots language). But the stance is taken in a universal context. The whole cosmos is going to have to adjust to accommodate these characters.

It's a country poem, and MacDiarmid is not primarily a poet of the city. In 'Dìreadh II' he pictures himself in the countryside,

> ... looking
> Over the blue waters of Loch Rannoch
> To the whole snow-capped range
> Of the Grampians and Cairngorms

– and declares this to be 'the real Scotland' as opposed to 'Edinburgh and Glasgow, which are rubbish'. Nevertheless, even a poem entitled 'In the Slums of Glasgow' (pp.201–4) closes with lines vividly evoking a kind of vision of hope: the sounds of a city's factories and workplaces winding down as the city-dweller lies at rest with his beloved.

> There is no movement but your eyelashes fluttering
>   against me,
> And the fading sound of the work-a-day world,
> Dadadoduddadaddadi dadadodudadidadoh,
> Duddadam dadade dudde dadadadadadodadah.

Language itself, attempting a hopeful communication, was MacDiarmid's central concern throughout his work, from the early lyrics on. In 'Ex Vermibus' (pp.10–11) the bird feeding worms to its fledglings promises that such nourishment will inspire them to 'a slee and sliggy sang' (a sly, cunning song) and 'byous spatrils' (wonderful musical sounds) as they fly over the tree-tops all day long. The poem's language is its own 'sliggy sang' and the sense of the language of poetry being essentially musical (the poem as song) is never far away.

Like Nietzsche, MacDiarmid is a thinker with a sense of humour, a relish for argument, an appetite for intellectual ideas, and a commitment to the individual will and its potential to create change, to break free of predestined patterns and con-formity. Like Nietzsche, irreverence helps him see through his own pretensions. He might shock and disgust his readers, rather than offer them contemplation; laughter is important to him and no subject is sacred. In 'Lourd on My Hert' (pp.125–6) the proverbially unending wintriness of the Scottish weather is jokily linked to the moment of the crucifixion.

Along with this ironic humour, MacDiarmid follows Nietzsche in rejecting Western culture's denigration of the body as a source of sin and error, and reinstating the body as the ground of meaning and knowledge, capable of more than merely a will to survive, innately driven by a will to control its own world, a will to power. In *A Drunk Man Looks at the Thistle*, MacDiarmid evokes the sexual energies of the body in the memory of the wedding night, with the bride's

> Nerves in stounds o' delight,
> Muscles in pride o' power,
> Bluid as wi' roses dight
> Life's toppin' pinnacles owre
> (ll.477–80, p.42)

The body is yoked to the spirit:

> I wish I kent the physical basis
> O' a' life's seemin' airs and graces.
>
> It's queer the thochts a kittled cull [tickled testicles]
> Can raise, or splairgin' glit [ejaculating sperm] annul.
> (ll.581–4, p.46)

This fankle of spirit and matter takes place in the overlap between tragic despair and comic release, the conflicts and confusions of Apollo and Dionysos, the arena where 'extremes meet' in which MacDiarmid claims he will dwell for ever, avoiding reassurance or certainty, accepting all objections and non sequiturs:

> I'll bury nae heid like an ostrich's,
> Nor yet believe my een and naething else.
> My senses may advise me, but I'll be
> Mysel' nae maitter what they tell's ...
> (ll.145–8, p.31)

For he has no faith in anything he can explain, he says, and therefore starts 'whaur the philosophers leave aff ...'

Above all he presents himself as a poet of Scotland, whose love of the whole country was tested and deepened by his knowledge of its various parts and the diversity of its peoples. He lived in almost every corner of the country, and in poems like 'Scotland' (pp.229–30), 'Scotland Small?' (p.230) or 'A Vision of Scotland' (p.264) he describes national identity as a multifaceted coherence. Thinking of Scotland, he once wrote, is like looking into water where the depth becomes so great it seems to move and swell without the slightest ripple, but gives a strange sense of 'the sun's stability'.

For all the diversity, however, his poems are deeply optimistic declarations of hope. He never lost faith in people and he believed that with imagination, appetite and energy, the people of Scotland should keep faith with themselves, to be true to what might yet be created in the world. His poems face up to the most serious questions and confront despair and loneliness, fearful disease and death; they are never simplistic, but they are almost all fundamentally hopeful.

from *A Drunk Man Looks at the Thistle*: 'Sic Transit Gloria Scotiae' (ll.1–60, pp.26–7)

A Drunk Man Looks at the Thistle begins by warning us not to believe what we're told. The title has promised us the view of a drunk man but the first words tell us that the first person singular is not so much drunk as exhausted, tired out from the work involved in drinking rather than drunk on alcohol or anything else. The voice is deflated and collapsing (beautifully caught in the onomatopoeia of 'deid dune'), satiated with the effort of being in supposedly convivial company. The opening line is an echo of a song by Robert Burns, 'Willie brew'd a peck o' maut': 'We are na fou, we're nae that fou ...' – so even the seemingly direct statement conceals an oblique reference, suggesting again that more is going on here than can be seen on the surface.

As the tone descends into complaint, a familiar whine is heard about the worth of whisky going down as its price has risen. Like everything else called 'Scotch' or 'Scottish' these days, there is no real spirit in it.

So far the grousing has been fairly low-key and unemphatic. Now a parenthesis opens and within the brackets a new tone is heard, more confiding, sly and insinuating. The so-called drunk man, the first person of the poem, openly declares what he's planning to go on to do. Prompted by the reference to national identity, he says he's going to prove his 'soul' is Scots by beginning with the obvious things – what everybody expects and thinks of when they think of the word. But then he'll move up to higher things 'by visible degrees' – in other words, he'll make it very clear when he rises from the clichés and the caricatures to matters which have nothing of heather, haggis or tartan about them. And once he has lured his readers into these realms, he promises to throw them back down into the depths of banality. As an explanation, he simply says, there is no choice: anyone, any person, man or woman, should wish 'To dree the goat's weird tae as weel's the sheep's': to suffer the fate of the goat, as well as that of the sheep. What does that mean? The goat is traditionally an animal associated with the Devil in Christian mythology, and 'the goat's weird' – the fate of the goat – means the destiny of the damned. The sheep are the lambs of God, the saved, devout Christians, the redeemed.

In Christian mythology good and evil are opposite terms, opposed to each other diametrically. The conventional teaching of the Christian Church is to be good, to reject evil. This is only one mythology, though. In ancient Greek religion and mythology Dionysos (the principle of the irrational and unpredictable, god of wine and intoxication) was as vital as Apollo (god of reason, light and measurement). In that pregnant line 'To dree the goat's weird tae as weel's the sheep's', MacDiarmid is rejecting the Christian ethos and saying that however much anyone would wish to deny it, it is the fate of any human being to be *both* damned *and* saved, to know the good and the bad, the drunk and sober, the mad and the sane, to be part of spirit, part of matter, to feel the flesh pulse and give, and fail and decay: and that that is as it should be.

Exclamation mark. Close brackets. New stanza. Shift of tone, shift of everything: now the words are of a different kind, names – Heifitz, Harry Lauder, Isadora Duncan, Mary Garden and Duncan Grant. What's happening?

These references might have been familiar at one time, and to some people they still are. They're the names of specialists: Jascha Heifitz was a violinist who played in concert halls throughout the world to great acclaim – he wore tartan when he was on stage with Harry Lauder; Lauder was an immensely popular singer and comedian; Mary Garden was a soprano, a Scottish vocalist who devoted her life to the art she was serving; Duncan Grant was a painter, an artist whose name and works are referred to even now in histories of English or British, but not Scottish, art; Isadora Duncan was a famous choreographer and dancer. The point about all this is simply that the caricatures and clichés – tartan (Heifitz), meanness and sniggering humour (associated with Lauder) – are one version of lowbrow 'Scottishness' recognised internationally, but others – Duncan Grant, Isadora Duncan, Mary Garden – are not recognisably Scottish – they don't conform to the caricatures – but they're active in ways that have everything to do with creativity and nothing to do with nationalism. And beyond all these famous people, there is the comical, self-explosive, reductive, giveaway last phrase: they're all very busy, and I'm here, drunk. The stanza ends with a question mark, but it's a rhetorical question, expecting no answer.

'Thus the glory of Scotland passes away' is the meaning of the Latin tag that opens the next stanza: all the best creative work that comes from Scots is taken out of Scotland altogether, denationalised. The flowers of the forest are all cut down. This is a reference to the song 'The Flowers of the Forest' by Jean Elliot and the beautiful lament, the tune which accompanies it. If you've read

Lewis Grassic Gibbon's novel *Sunset Song*, the first of his great
trilogy *A Scots Quair*, you'll know that it ends with the minister's
sermon for those who died in World War I. ('They died for a world
that is past, these men, but they did not die for this that we seem
to inherit.') The assembled company listen to the piper McIvor play
the lament and Gibbon goes so far as to print the music on a page
of his novel: 'it lifted your hair and was eerie and uncanny'. It's a
well-known tune, frequently played at funerals or occasions of
communal mourning. MacDiarmid cites it here along with the
Latin phrase almost ironically, using once again that deflated,
exhausted tone with which the poem began. Then another set of
brackets opens: is there a possibility that a blind bird is building a
new nest in the branches of the thistle? Presumably the bird would
have to be blind if it chose the thistle to build a nest in, and if the
thistle stands for Scotland maybe MacDiarmid is referring to
himself, hoping to hatch a new set of fledglings in this spiky
environment. But he doesn't linger on this notion. It's just as well
the bird is blind if its offspring are as useless as all the others, he
says. Close parenthesis. Back to direct speech. And now we're on
familiar ground again with references to Robert Burns and Burns
suppers.

There's a ferocious, rippling eloquence to the angry language of
these next stanzas (ll.37–60). With unstoppable, indiscriminate
hostility, they set about slaughtering the hypocrisy and
pretentiousness of the people – probably all men, in the 1920s –
who attend Burns suppers, from London to 'Bagdad', making
after-dinner speeches in their best suits, knowing next to nothing
of what Burns actually wrote and regurgitating conventionally
acceptable 'sloppy rubbish' every year. The parodies of Chinese
speech ('Him Haggis – velly goot!') and posh English (the 'London
Scotties' rejoice that there are 'similah gatherings in Timbuctoo')
are justly brutal and MacDiarmid is encouraging a healthily
derisive laughter at all this humbug, snobbery and ignorance. But
underneath that there's a tragic sense of the wastefulness of so
much effort, surrounding 'Genius' with the thoughts of these
nincompoops. Burns, Liberty and Christ are the three words
which seem to have triggered more spurious sermons and
speeches than any others. If this keeps spreading (and the feeling
is that it probably will), 'as the drink declines / Syne turns to tea'
(that reference links back to the opening remarks about whisky
no longer being as good as it used to be), then 'wae's me for the
Zeitgeist!' That last phrase is a terrific compression of tones,
mock-melodramatic ('Woe is me! How dreadful! I despair!') and

mock-high serious: *Zeitgeist* means the spirit of the age and the German gives it a solemnity and straight-faced seriousness which refers to a seminal book of the period, Oswald Spengler's *Decline of the West*, which prophesied the decay and end of Western civilization. 'Wae's me for the *Zeitgeist!*' indeed.

How might these first pages of the poem be described generally? After the exhausted opening lines, there's a racy, rushing, vertiginous velocity and then there are sudden transformations: not a single dull line or unnecessary phrase; everything is working. A continual sense of play, a lusty engagement with ideas, people, events, references, things, combines with a sense of humour, of sharp critical hostility, and at least potentially a generosity of sympathy underlying the cantankerous impatience. You might look back over the first fifteen stanzas now that we've gone through them (or forward through the next fourteen, pp.28–9) and try to find appropriate quotations that would fit the qualities just listed. As we know, however, the comedy of the early pages of the poem gives way to much more mysterious, serious and sinister tones, unearthly lights and wonderments.

But MacDiarmid can be a very funny writer, with a zany, irrepressible and irreverent sense of humour. It's more evident in some of his stories and sketches: in the *Selected Prose*, for example, there are richly layered ironies in 'The Dour Drinkers of Glasgow', an almost surreal portrait of village life in 'The Waterside' and a devastating satire in 'The Last Great Burns Discovery'. MacDiarmid's comedy is generous and instantly recognisable. It is, perhaps, the key to his work.

There are, of course, different kinds of humour. Comedy takes many forms: there are jokes, involving wordplay, puns, deliberate mistakes; there's the comedy of bathos, when the unexpected happens and the result is startlingly incongruous; there's the comedy of the absurd and inexplicable (like the discovery of a right-hand glove which was never reported lost, in which a full set of thumb- and finger-nails was found quietly rattling, recounted in 'The Dour Drinkers of Glasgow'); there's the comedy of disgust or 'horripilation' in 'Five Bits of Miller' (the five bits are his mucus, blackheads, nails, phlegm and earwax); there's the comedy of social satire, or of festivity and celebration, which might involve ritual (seasonal events) or particular occasions (birthdays or special moments) and MacDiarmid wrote numerous 'occasional' poems for friends or to commemorate particular events, like the 1948 'A Birthday Wish to T.S. Eliot' or the poem on the 'Royal Visit' to Scotland in 1953, or the celebratory poem for the 1962 opening of Brecht's *The Good Woman of Szechuan* at the Citizen's Theatre, Glasgow.

MacDiarmid's comic poems aren't always frivolous, however. Norman MacCaig once remarked that usually in the work of English writers comedy and seriousness were kept in separate categories, but in MacDiarmid's work, and indeed in the work of many Scottish writers, from Henryson and Dunbar, through Burns, Hogg, Scott and pre-eminently Byron, to the twentieth century, comedy and humour are often to be found aiding and abetting a serious argument. The qualities of humour and seriousness are intertwined and inseparable. So it is with MacDiarmid's poems.

'Old Wife in High Spirits' (pp.304–5)

'Old Wife in High Spirits' is located 'In an Edinburgh Pub' and unusually for MacDiarmid, it's almost entirely a narrative poem, telling a story about what happens to a particular character in a particular situation. It's not until the seventh and final stanza that a first person singular appears, though the voice of the observer is heard clearly in the penultimate stanza too, making a moral and ethical pronouncement on the events just described. This might seem rather pontifical, a 'judgement from on high', yet it's clear that the voice is in sympathy with the old woman, and the fiery spirit that runs through her; and by the end of the poem the tone is one of respect and admiration, as well as sympathy.

There is no psychological characterisation as such. No sentimental wish to make her seem exceptional as an individual is present; she is simply an 'Old Wife' (she could be *any* 'Old Wife'), and the implication of the word 'Wife' (that she is or has been married, has had children and having seen them grow up and leave, is facing old age in the wake of her family's departure) speaks of the assumption of the social world the woman – and the poet – come from. However constrained and exhausting that world might be, the key to releasing its capacity for abundant ('muckle') life is there in the pun in the poem's title ('Spirits' means both alcoholic liquor and emotive energy); it's also overwhelmingly present in the poem's language.

The poem (like 'Crowdieknowe') belongs to the tradition of 'comic resurrection' in which someone apparently dead or nearly dead ('a mere rickle o' banes' suggests the skeleton beneath the skin) is revived. The Irish ballad 'Finnegan's Wake' is the most famous example, since James Joyce resurrected its title (minus the apostrophe) for his final work, a summation of the 'comic resurrection' tradition. Drink often has a part to play in such resurrection and after the description of the old wife ('you'd think she could haurdly ha'e had less / Life left in her and still lived'), the next character to be introduced is the publican – referred to without further explanation simply as 'He'. The publican introduces the third element: the catalyst, the whisky that reverses expectations and turns the situation inside out. After a couple of drams and a shared joke, the rock of politeness and correct behaviour is split and the wild 'nature' springs up.

The language now moves very quickly and the exercise of reading the poem aloud is exhilarating, demanding an enthusiastic engagement of voice, throat, muscle, lips and saliva, a bodily but precise articulation.

The celebration enacted by the poem isn't just a release of happy laughter. With one drink over the eight, 'her temper changed' and her angry voice flies like lightning.

The Welsh poet Dylan Thomas has a passionate poem protesting against the death of his father, 'Do Not Go Gentle Into That Good Night', in which he cries out for 'Rage, rage against the dying of the light'. MacDiarmid's poem catches an aspect of that rage but the volcanic energy released in it is explosively expressive, very different from the implosive anguish of Thomas's despairing anger. Once that energy has been evoked (the old wife 'fair in her element; / Wanton as a whirlwind') the moral judgement of the poet begins to enter the tone: '... and shairly better that way / Than a' crippen thegither wi' laneliness and cauld ...'

It's as if the poet were witnessing these events, sitting in the pub, off to one side. This position is assumed from the opening: 'An auld wumman cam' in ...' That phrase locates the speaker (and, imaginatively, the reader) inside the pub from the start. The 'moral' of the story might seem like an intrusion, but it's also a reversal or subversion of traditional moral conclusions in parables, for example. Christian piety and the bourgeois desire for property and comfort are rejected. The contempt in the tone of 'Ninety per cent o' respectable folk' can be clearly heard in the syllables of 'respectable' and the alliteration of 'r' and 's' sounds. This is the MacDiarmid who, at the end of his magnificently wayward 'autobiography', wrote:

> And my last word here is that, if I had to choose a
> motto to be engraved under my name and the dates
> of my birth and death on my tombstone, it would be:
> 'A disgrace to the community.' – Mr Justice Mugge.

'The Ross-shire Hills' (p.306)

A poem in plain English, a simple rhyme-scheme (ABCB, DEFE) and eight marvellously varied four-stress lines (the stresses fall in different parts of each line according to the syntax, so reading the poem is an unpredictable, 'wanchancy' thing). For example, the stresses in line 1 fall regularly on 'What' 'hills' 'Ross-' and 'like' but in line 2, they fall on the first, one-word sentence: 'Listen' – and 'tell' in the second, three-word sentence, and on 'snow' and 'day' in the third, five-word sentence which moves at a much longer, flowing, yet brisk pace. The briskness continues in line 3 with a determined, 'gung-ho!' pitch on the words 'went' ('I *went* out') and 'gun' ('with my *gun*'). The full stop after the monosyllabic 'gun' gives it extra, disingenuous, firm emphasis. The sequence of events is almost predictable: what else *could* happen next other than a hare popping up? And there's a wonderful, cartoon-like quality here, an absurdity in the end-of-line focus: 'A hare popped up' which can be savoured across lines 3 and 4, through the enjambment, to 'On a hill-top' (the internal rhyme on 'pop' and 'top' suggesting a delightful childish simplicity in its uncomplicated immediacy). And the final phrase 'not very far away' almost implies an ellipsis of three dots, rather than a full stop, to follow, because the stanza-break creates a momentary tension: the sequence of events or the narrative of the poem is hanging suspended, suspenseful, as we move to the second stanza.

Again, the short sentence is direct, unfussy, almost brutally self-assured (no pious anti-blood sports feeling here): 'I shot it at once.' And again, the movement over the second half of line 5, on and into line 6, exactly matches the rolling downhill movement it describes and the unusual sense of gathering momentum and, mysteriously, the simultaneous sense of an accretion of weight, gathering packed snow: 'It came rolling down / And round it as it came a snowball grew'. The absence of punctuation in that line is a perfect illustration of how carefully the voice is modulating this language, for there are brief pauses, unwritten commas, after 'it' and 'came' ('as it came' is a kind of unemphatic parenthesis in the line: 'And round it[,] as it came[,] a snowball grew,' – each three-word phrase enacts a small rolling sound), and the final comma shunts your eye round to the penultimate line, where the commas are indeed put to work, slowing the reading down: 'Which, when I kicked it open, held not one' – and onto the last line, the punch-line of the joke, given quickly, over almost before you know it, then backed up by two more short knockout little sentences and the final rhyme-word (both an assurance of conviction and, simultaneously, an expression of helpless wonder in the face of the inexplicable and marvellous): '... not one / But seventeen hares. Believe me or not. It's true.'

Simplicity itself. Nothing could be more straightforward. So you might think. But you've always got to be careful with poems.

In Memoriam James Joyce gives you the clue: 'all this here, everything I write, of course / Is an extended metaphor for something I never mention' (p.272). And that's true of 'The Ross-shire Hills'. He tells you as much at the start: 'What are the hills of Ross-shire like? / Listen. I'll tell you.' What he tells us is a wee story that is meant to show us what these hills, this place, is 'like': it's a magical place, where singular becomes plural, where the unseen makes an appearance, where the sparse, barren winter landscape becomes abundant with life – and food for the pot.

Ross-shire, one of Scotland's ancient provinces, is in the north, including Highland and Hebridean areas in the west and crossing the Highland line in the east; it is perhaps the one district in which might be found almost all the constituent parts of Scotland's multifarious character: geographically, linguistically, culturally and historically. So 'The Ross-shire Hills' is perhaps a metaphor for Scotland as a whole. But this isn't in any sense a jingoistic nationalist poem; it's also a metaphor for something much more universal.

In the end, it's a metaphor and a parable about human creativity, the process of art. It's about setting out with a firm purpose to do one thing – and doing something more. It's about serendipity, the happy, unexpected discovery that there's more in life than prediction can quantify, there's something that cannot be calculated. But you can count on it: in the Ross-shire hills, in Scotland, and in the poetry of Hugh MacDiarmid.

4. Advanced Study

In Memoriam James Joyce is such a radical departure from what many people consider poetry should be, that a general introduction to its themes and methods is probably required. Before you begin to consider its substance and terrain, of course, you should read the work itself in its entirety, preferably in one session: that way its scope and scale are unmistakable. After that, we might convey some of our enthusiasm and a little knowledge more effectively. *In Memoriam James Joyce* is where MacDiarmid expresses the optimism he earned through his long and arduous career with the fullest range of reference and variety of forms.

In Memoriam James Joyce (pp.272–98)

The first thing to understand about *In Memoriam James Joyce* is that it isn't a poem. It's poetry, but it doesn't conform to normal ideas about what a poem should be. Usually a poem is taken to mean something coherent and structurally unified, a balanced artifact in which a first person singular, a persona, an 'I' utters a speech in a language that is deliberately 'heightened' or 'special'. But in MacDiarmid's Joyce poem there are large passages of material quoted from other people's writing, transformed from prose into verse, and embedded in the work, often without acknowledgement. Reading *In Memoriam James Joyce* is like an exhilarating journey on foot across a mountain range. There's a lot of hard work involved but the views can be tremendous and there's real pleasure in making the trip, and achievement in having made it.

In Memoriam James Joyce works, not by any sense of *governing certainty* controlled by a *lyrical ego*, but by *obtrusions of parentheses* and *intrusions of meaning*. If we can call it a poem at all it is a poem given coherence by our act of reading it – not in any formal structure it possesses in itself. Although it's possible to describe what happens in *In Memoriam James Joyce* and to sense a movement from the recurrent concern with language and the world of words in the early part of the book, to the language of music in the latter part, that shape seems almost a discovery the poem makes for itself in the course of our reading it. The connections between individual sections sometimes seem arbitrary and undeveloped. Occasionally it's as if MacDiarmid is simply taking notes; the syntax breaks down; another bracket opens and the logic seems to work through the parentheses rather than around them.

What we're now calling 'the poem' should strictly be called 'the book'. *In Memoriam James Joyce* was the title of a book published in 1955, containing six sections. The first was actually called 'In Memoriam James Joyce'. Then came 'The World of Words', 'The Snares of Varuna', 'The Meeting of the East and the West' and 'England Is our Enemy'. The final section was called 'Plaited like the Generations of Men' and begins 'Come, follow me into the realm of music ...'

MacDiarmid began writing what was to become this book in the 1930s. He hoped to bring all his poetry together on an epic scale, in one, great, coherent masterwork, the longest, most comprehensive poem ever written in the English language (or at least, using English as a predominant medium).

Each specific area which MacDiarmid brings into the orbit of his later poetry probably could be corrected by a suitably qualified professional specialist, but their effect should be to send an enquiring mind back out from the poetry to the separate disciplines, empowered with the conviction that they are all inter-related and ultimately interdependent. MacDiarmid was committed to his belief in humanity's 'common interest' politically, and correspondingly, he believed that all subject areas, including the sciences, were the material of poetry. So in 'Direadh III' (pp.231–9), there is a transcription from the writing of the genetic biologist, H.J. Muller (on p.238), and the opening of 'Plaited like the Generations of Men' comes from a letter of the composer Ferruccio Busoni, and a little later (pp.296–7) there's a passage from the scientist J.B.S. Haldane about the nature of biological evolution that seems to take place while the foetus is growing in the womb.

Every crisis in art is a crisis of form, and MacDiarmid's later poetry represents that crisis again and again. It is most concisely stated in this extract from *The Battle Continues* (p.222):

> One loves the temporal, some unique manifestation,
> Something irreplaceable that dies.
>
> But one is loyal to an ideal limit
> Involved in all specific objects of love
> And in all cooperating wills.
>
> Shall the lonely griefs and joys of men
> Forever remain a pluralistic universe?
> Need they, if thought and will are bent in common interest
> In making this universe *one*?

The political dimension of MacDiarmid's later work is crucial, for it is all essentially concerned with the relations between language, poetry and imperialism. Those relations are his work's *subject*. Language he considers in its widest possible sense: all forms of communication, from the most obscure and ancient tongues to modern slang, the 'languages' of other media (film, dance, painting, specialist scientific discourses). Poetry similarly means more than one thing in terms of specific forms, 'the temporal, some unique manifestation' – but in the most general sense the word 'poetry' registers value, something that operates on a different, more intense, more acutely felt register: 'Poetry is human existence come to life' (p.274). And imperialism is the great enemy for MacDiarmid precisely because it signifies absolute control of all those forms of expression and the ruthless suppression of the most 'negligible' or less 'important' forms: ' – All dreams of "imperialism" must be exorcised, / Including linguistic imperialism, which sums up all the rest' (p.276).

He felt this personally in the imperial authority commanded by the English language, in school when he was a boy; he felt it even more desperately as it applied to Gaelic, which had been outlawed and relegated to a minority of the Scottish population, and was horribly stigmatised by Anglocentric imperialist assumptions of superiority. He felt it intellectually, happening all over the colonial world, in the persecution of minority languages and minority cultures.

In Memoriam James Joyce begins in the international 'world of words' as a celebration of the richness of expressive diversity, but it ends having passed through 'the gate / Which separates the earthly from the eternal'. This is, perhaps, the ultimate declaration of faith in the world:

> The heart of each separate living thing
> Beats differently, according to its needs,
> And all the beats are in harmony.
> (p.286)

This assertion comes in the aftermath of two world wars and out of appalling personal isolation. It's a claim to answer the atrocities of the twentieth century with a human response profoundly engaged with language, but reaching receptively beyond its temporality to 'the realm of music'.

> Each sound is the centre of endless circles,
> And now the *harmony* opens out before you.
> Innumerable are its voices ...
> (p.287)

This belief in an eternal harmony in music that might be heard beyond, but also in, the human voice and other earthly sounds has been made before in MacDiarmid's work, but never with such total commitment.

By the time we have reached the end of *In Memoriam James Joyce*, the journey will have equipped us with a range and depth of experience and an artillery of references which we still have to learn how to use familiarly. They all bear lightly upon the final phrases of farewell (p.298). These come from the ancient Roman poet Horace (65–8 B.C.): *'Non me rebus subjungere conor!'* ('I won't let things get the better of me!') and the proverbial Gurkhali phrase, used by dockers in Indian seaports when cargoes disastrously slipped overboard by accident: 'Don't worry, boss: everything's really okay': *'Sab thik chha'*.

It's an affirmation that brings antiquity and modernity into alignment, the worlds of high learning and low speech, different sounds, related in harmony, as carnal and as lasting as the affirmation which concludes Joyce's own great work of vernacular and classical resolution, *Ulysses*: 'yes I said yes I will Yes.'

Further Reference

Bibliography

Works by Hugh MacDiarmid

The Letters of Hugh MacDiarmid, edited by Alan Bold (London: Hamish Hamilton, 1984)

A Drunk Man Looks at the Thistle, edited by Kenneth Buthlay (Edinburgh: Scottish Academic Press, 1987)

Selected Prose, edited by Alan Riach (Manchester: Carcanet Press, 1992)

Complete Poems (2 volumes), edited by Michael Grieve and W.R. Aitken (Manchester: Carcanet Press, 1993–4)

Selected Poems, edited by Alan Riach and Michael Grieve (Harmondsworth: Penguin Books, 1994)

Lucky Poet, edited by Alan Riach (Manchester: Carcanet Press: 1994)

Albyn: Shorter Books and Monographs, edited by Alan Riach (Manchester: Carcanet Press: 1996)

The Raucle Tongue: Hitherto Uncollected Prose (3 volumes), edited by Angus Calder, Glen Murray and Alan Riach (Manchester: Carcanet Press: 1996–8)

Critical and Biographical Works

Alan Bold, *MacDiarmid: Christopher Murray Grieve: A Critical Biography* (London: Paladin, 1990)

Kenneth Buthlay, 'The Appreciation of the Golden Lyric: Early Scots Poems of Hugh MacDiarmid', *Scottish Literary Journal*, 2:1 (July 1975), pp.41–66

Kenneth Buthlay, 'Some Hints for Source-hunters', *Scottish Literary Journal*, 5:2 (December 1978), pp.50–66

Kenneth Buthlay, *Hugh MacDiarmid* (Edinburgh: Scottish Academic Press, 1982)

Kenneth Buthlay, 'The Ablach in the Gold Pavilion', *Scottish Literary Journal*, 15:2 (November 1988), pp.39–57

David Daiches, 'Hugh MacDiarmid's Early Poetry', in *Hugh MacDiarmid: A Critical Survey*, edited by Duncan Glen (Edinburgh and London: Scottish Academic Press, 1972), pp.58–84

Laurence Graham and Brian Smith, editors, *MacDiarmid in Shetland* (Lerwick: Shetland Library, 1992)

Seamus Heaney, 'A Torchlight Procession of One: On Hugh MacDiarmid', in *The Redress of Poetry: Oxford Lectures* (London: Faber and Faber, 1995), pp.103–23

Walter Perrie, *Out of Conflict* (Dunfermline: Borderline, 1982)

TLS: Essays and Reviews from the Times Literary Supplement, volume 4: 1965 (London, 1966): 'Mr MacDiarmid and Dr Grieve', pp.176–95

Alan Riach, *Hugh MacDiarmid's Epic Poetry* (Edinburgh: Edinburgh University Press, 1991)

Alan Riach, 'The Idea of Order and "On a Raised Beach": The Language of Location and the Politics of Music', in *Terranglian Territories*, edited by Susanne Hagemann (Frankfurt am Main: Peter Lang, 2000)

Marshall Walker, *Scottish Literature Since 1707* (Harlow: Longman, 1996)

Roderick Watson, *MacDiarmid* (Milton Keynes: Open University Press, 1985)

Other Works

John Berger, *The Moment of Cubism and other essays* (London: Weidenfield and Nicolson, 1969)

Calum I. MacLean, *The Highlands* (London: Batsford, 1959)

Duncan MacMillan, *Scottish Art 1460–1990* (Edinburgh: Mainstream, 1990)

Andrew Marr, *The Battle for Scotland* (Harmondsworth: Penguin Books, 1992)

John Purser, *Scotland's Music: A History of the Traditional and Classical Music of Scotland from Earliest Times to the Present Day* (Edinburgh: Mainstream, 1992)

Adrian Poole, *Tragedy: Shakespeare and the Greek Example* (Oxford: Basil Blackwell, 1987)

'The Dead Liebknecht' by Rudolf Leonhardt

All through the city lies the corpse of him,
in all courtyards, in all streets,
with his outpoured blood
all chambers have grown dim.

Now the sirens of the factories begin
their yawning drone,
endlessly long,
over the whole city their hollow noise they spin.

And with a glimmer
of keen
bright teeth,
his corpse is seen
to smile.

From *Contemporary German Poetry: An Anthology* (1923), chosen and translated by Babette Deutsch and Avrahm Yarmolinsky.

Milkwort and Bog-cotton

HUGH MAC DIARMID

FRANCIS GEORGE SCOTT

frae the lift nae shadow can fa'_Since there's nocht left to thraw a shadow there_Owre een like milkwort

___ and milk-white cotton hair.   Wad that nae leaf up-on a_nither wheeled A shadow

either and nae root need dern_ In sac-ri-fice to let_ sic beau_ty be!___ But

deep sur‑roond‑in' dark‑ness I dis‑cern— Is aye the price o' licht.

Wad licht re‑vealed Naething but you, ——— and nicht nocht else

con‑cealed. ———